FAITH SEEKING
UNDERSTANDING

Leaving Certificate
Religious Education
Syllabus Section J

Religion and Science

Writers: Joseph McCann
& Fachtna McCarthy

Series Coordinator and Editor:
Micheál de Barra

Published 2006 by
Veritas Publications
7-8 Lower Abbey Street
Dublin 1

ISBN 1 84730 015 4
978 1 84730 015 7 (from January 2007)
Copyright © 2006 Irish Episcopal Commission on Catechetics
Printed with Ecclesiastical Approval

The writers and the editor would like to acknowledge the Religious Education teachers and students who piloted draft versions of this text and helped enormously with their feedback and comments. The would also like to thank the Post-Primary Diocesan Advisers for their invaluable help and support.

Theological Adviser: Pat Mullins OCarm STD
Consultant to the Series: Maura Hyland
Art Director: Bill Bolger
Design: Susan Waine and Colette Dower
Text Editor: Elaine Campion
Typesetting: Colette Dower
Copyright Research: Ruth Garvey and Caitriona Clarke
Origination: Digital Prepress Imaging
Printed in the Republic of Ireland by Betaprint Ltd, Dublin

Acknowledgements

Scripture quotations from the *New Revised Standard Version Bible* © 1993 and 1998 by the Division of Christian Education of the National Council of the Churches of Christ in the United States of America. Extract from 'Poem from a Three-Year-Old' (p.6) b Brendan Kennelly from *Familiar Strangers: New and Selected Poems, 1960-2004*, Bloodaxe Books, 2004, used with permission. 'Fire and Ice' by Robert Frost (p.109) from *The Poetry of Robert Frost: The Collected Poems, Complete and Unabridged* (Robert Frost and Edwa Connery Lathem), courtesy of Henry Holt and Company Inc., 1969.

Stock photography courtesy of www.sxc.hu; images of Bertrand Russell and Isaac Newton courtesy of Mary Evans Picture Libra (pp.13 and 18); 'Galileo and Milton' by Annibale Gatti (second half of 19th century) is reproduced with kind permission of Isstit e Museo di Storia della Scienza (p.50); 'Galileo Galilei (1564-1642) before members of the Holy Office in the Vatican in 1633', 1847 by Robert Fleury, Joseph Nicolas (1797-1890), Louvre, Paris, France/Peter Willi/The Bridgeman Art Library, Nationality/copyright, status: French/out of copyright (p.56); images of Robert Boyle, Pierre Laplace, Jean-Pierre Lamarck and Thomas Malthus courtesy of Mary Evans Picture Library (pp.70, 72, 77 and 78); image of Victorian cotton mills courtesy of Mar Evans Picture Library (p.85); photograph of mosque courtesy of Saleem Bhimji at www.sxc.hu (p.95); images of Albert Einstein Nils Bohr, Werner Heisenberg and Erwin Schrödinger courtesy of Mary Evans Picture Library (pp.120, 124, 125 and 126); 'Creation of Adam', detail from the Sistine Ceiling, 1511-12 (fresco) by Michelangelo Buonarroti (1475-1564), Vatican Museums and Galleries, Vatican City, Italy/The Bridgeman Art Library, Nationality/copyright status: Italian/out of copyright (p.143); imag supplied by Jeff Terry at www.sxc.hu (p.151); images on pages 160, 162 and 163 supplied by Getty Images.

Every effort has been made to contact the copyright holders of the material reproduced in *Religion and Science*. If any infringemer of copyright has occurred, the owners of such copyright are requested to contact the publishers.

Contents

Come, my friends,
'Tis not too late to seek a newer world.
Push off, and sitting well in order smite
The sounding furrows; for my purpose holds
To sail beyond the sunset, and the baths
Of all the western stars, until I die.
It may be that the gulfs will wash us down:
It may be we shall touch the Happy Isles,
And see the great Achilles, whom we knew.
Tho' much is taken, much abides; and tho'
We are not now that strength which in old days
Moved earth and heaven; that which we are, we are;
One equal temper of heroic hearts,
Made weak by time and fate, but strong in will
To strive, to seek, to find, and not to yield.

ALFRED LORD TENNYSON, *Ulysses*

Part 1: The Scientific and Theological Enterprises

Chapter 1

Questioning in Context

'And will the flowers die?
And will the people die?
And every day do you grow old, do I
grow old, no I'm not old, do
flowers grow old?'

Brendan Kennelly, *Poem from a Three-Year-Old*

In this chapter you will learn about...

...the human need to question. We will introduce the relationship between science and religion, and probe the reason why so many people think that they cannot mix. We explore WHY we would want to find out about the relationship between science and religion, and look at the kind of questions that science and religion ask. Finally, we will discuss the idea of questioning itself, and warn ourselves against giving over-simplified answers in science or religion.

Resources for further study
See teacher's text on CD-Rom for further suggestions.

INTRODUCTION

MAD SCIENTISTS

Very often, in films and TV programmes, scientists are presented as mad, power-crazy, unfeeling, absent-minded, 'egg-heads' detached from reality, in the American slang word, 'nerds'. Sometimes, of course, scientist characters are powerful, courageous and competent, but these examples are few enough. Commentators suggest that these extremes reveal a public awareness that is uneasy about science and what scientists do, and that this anxiety runs deep.

This topic is also considered in Section A, The Search for Meaning and Values and Section C, World Religions.

We call these exaggerated prejudiced and one-sided pictures 'caricatures'. Caricatures are cartoon versions of people. We can also call them 'stereotypes'. **Stereotypes** of scientists are deplorable because they encourage an unthinking reaction to science and scientists by the public. The absent-minded professor, the mad experimenter, the power-hungry Doctor No are examples that colour people's attitudes, obscuring the contribution that science makes to modern life. The result is that science is not respected for its contributions to modern life.

1. How do you and your friends feel about science? Would you be happy in a scientific job? Find out how many of your friends and classmates are seriously considering a scientific career.

2. Educators and governments are worried that not enough young people are interested in scientific careers. What do you think? What is your (and your friends') experience in that regard?

Yet the reality is that in every area of modern living, science has made things better, easier and cheaper. We live in a comfort and luxury unimagined by previous ages, and the application of science has made it possible. The promise of science is that these benefits may be shared with everyone on the planet.

COMIC CLERGY

The media also stereotype religious people of all kinds: priests, nuns, vicars, gurus and so on. In the past, priests and ministers were portrayed in films as compassionate, caring and committed. Your grandparents would remember Bing Crosby in *Going My Way*. But more recently, clergy and religious sisters in film and television are caricatured in a fashion similar to the treatment of scientists. Examples are *Father Ted* and *Sister Act*. Religious characters come across as dotty and soft-headed, emotional and childish, personable but trivial; in other words, figures of fun.

The modern world has pushed religious people to the margins. Religious people deal with the mystical, the spiritual, the personal, the private, the subjective and the emotional – areas seemingly unimportant for modern life. Often people see religion as being no more than a woolly thinking or airy speculation. This attitude may be found even among educated people, and not just at the level of popular conversation.

A BIT OF BALANCE

Caricatures of science and religion are both inaccurate. Scientists are not unfeeling, uncaring, inhuman and calculating 'brains on stilts'. Scientists are, in fact, rather a mixed lot, like human beings in general. Some scientists are conventional types; some are eccentric. Some scientists are geniuses, but many are just ordinary folk. Even where religious belief is concerned, scientists are pretty much the same as everyone else; there are some who are believers and some who are not.

The stereotype of the impractical and ignorant religious believer is as mistaken as that of the unbelieving scientist. Theologians and religious thinkers are not gullible flat-earthers, end-of-the-world dreamers, who are more poetical than practical. The Anglican archbishop John Habgood is a trained scientist. The Vatican employs its own astronomers and has its own observatory. Some of the botanists and naturalists who supported Darwin were Church of England clergymen.

We should also notice something very important about media representations: they never convey any real sense of what scientists or religious people actually do. The media seldom show nuns and clergy praying in a convincing manner, just as they seldom portray scientists carrying out any real research.

QUESTIONS FOR RELIGION AND SCIENCE

Our age requires us to explore nature as fully as we can, and it also asks us to use the resources of our world as justly and fairly as we can. People have to explore the capabilities of the planet, and at the same time pay heed to the needs of the human race. We need science and technology and an enthusiasm for discovery and experimentation in order to understand the world. We need philosophy and theology, ethical convictions, religious belief, contemplative awareness and devotion to the human community in order to nurture the human spirit. Humanity requires both. How important is the dialogue between science and religion for us all? There are two possible answers: one at the level of the individual and the other at the level of society.

Questions

1. Can you remember other stereotypical religious characters in films, TV programmes, advertisements, novels and stories or other media?
2. How do religious characters appear in the media with which you are familiar? What about MTV? Teen magazines? Soaps? Music?

Archbishop John Habgood

For discussion

1. How would you go about presenting a scientist actually practising science in a film, play or TV programme? What scenes would you show? What would you be trying to depict? Which qualities and experiences of the person do you think are important to emphasise?
2. How would you present a religious person in a similar situation? What scenes would you present? What would you be trying to depict? Which qualities and experiences of the religious person do you think are important to highlight?

First, the individual answer: All people want to know about their own life and destiny. We ask questions about where we have come from, and where we are going. We want to know what it all means. We are worried that life may not all add up in the end. Both science and religion offer explanations that answer these questions. Often we find that the answer offered by science is not the same as the answer from religion. So, we need to understand both science and religion in order to sort out our own minds on these important personal questions and their answers.

Second, the social answer: Our civilisation is facing very big decisions, about population control, use of natural resources, care of the environment, medical advances, care of the sick and elderly, new technologies and so on. The opportunities and dangers before us demand careful reflection and responsible decision-making. That means that we should be informed, aware of what is being thought and taught in both science and religion, because it is we who will be making these decisions.

PURPOSE FOR STUDYING RELIGION AND SCIENCE

An educated person, therefore, needs adequate information about science and religion, and an understanding of their relationship. The reason that you are learning about religion and science, then, is to provide this information and to give you a chance to discuss the relationship between them in some depth.

There are four parts to this section of the course:
● The nature and methods of the scientific and theological enterprises.
● The story of some key moments in the history of the relationship between religion and science.

Two of the emerging contemporary debates between religion and science:
● (i) the origin of the universe;
● (ii) important issues of life and death.

QUESTIONING IN CONTEXT

MAKING SENSE OF THINGS

Resources for further study
See teacher's text on CD-Rom for further suggestions.

John Macnamara, an Irish psychologist, wrote a fascinating book called *Names for Things*. In it, he describes the way infants learn how to name the things that they first encounter. He watched his own child in its first explorations, and noticed how he labelled the new things he met. It is not easy for the child to notice and record the names that others have attached

to things, then to remember the words and, finally, to recognise things when they meet them for a second time. The child must identify Rover as an individual dog. He also needs to know that Rover is called a 'dog' as well as 'Rover'. Then he has to recognise Rover tomorrow, and learn to refer to Rover as a 'dog' as well as call him 'Rover'. Finally, the child must learn to use the word 'dog', but not 'Rover', of all the other dogs in the world. This is no small task.

Psychologists are very interested in 'the child as scientist'. John Macnamara's young boy was such a scientist. He was questioning everything and everyone he met. What is this? What is it called? What does it do? Why? And so on. Scientists know this as categorisation and classification: the first duty of a scientist on meeting anything new. It is, of course, what we all do: question and interrogate our world to find out what is going on in it.

HUMAN NEED TO QUESTION

Humans will always try to make sense of their lives, because they are naturally curious about everything. That is the way that we are made. It is as if we are wired to ask questions, to investigate, to enquire about everything that happens to us.

In school, it may not look as if human beings are naturally curious. Sometimes (you may not agree) we feel we get too much knowledge at a time when we do not want it. All of us have had to learn more than we ever wanted to know about seeds, or quadratic equations, or the capital of Mongolia

For discussion

1. Do you remember your first questions about the world? Were they about plants and animals? Or were they about machines and things? Or about the past and the future? Perhaps they were about people and happenings, or about thoughts and feelings deep within?

2. Have you given up these questions as you grow up? Why? Would you like to start wondering again?

3. Have you watched or talked to a young child who is beginning to question the world? Have you tried to answer? What have you found out by trying to answer the child?

(which is Ulan Bator, in case you want to know!) This makes for young people who have been filled so full with unwanted information that they have temporarily lost the appetite for asking their own questions. The problem is that school gives us answers before we have the questions.

Nevertheless, all of us are naturally curious. And we are sure that we can find out the answers to our questions. Both of these sentences are important. Without the second, the first would be frustrating. To be very curious, and want to find out things, but at the same time to be unable to satisfy the curiosity, would mean that we are defective in one crucial element: our minds.

Twenty Questions
You and a few of your friends should try the game 'Twenty Questions'. One of you thinks of a person or animal, a plant or a thing. He or she tells the others only whether the object of thought is 'animal, vegetable or mineral'. Then the group has twenty questions to find out what it is. The questions must be answered only with 'Yes' or 'No'. Enjoy.

How did you do? How did the group do? There is no better illustration of the art of questioning. The fun part is that your questions have to be both effective and efficient: that is, you have to get the required information (be effective) in the least number of tries (be efficient). Questions in this game can only be answered with 'Yes' or 'No', so you must frame the question to derive the maximum benefit.

'Twenty Questions' also shows you how important it is to listen carefully to the answer, and to set it against information you already have in your possession. You do not want to ask a question twice or get the same information twice. Finally, you always need some idea of what the final answer might be – the

For discussion

1. It has been said that a person has to be at least twenty-five years old to be a philosopher, that is, to be interested in asking questions about the ultimate meaning of life. Would you agree with this?
2. Do you or your friends wonder about why you are alive?
3. Do you write poetry? What is it about?
4. Have you ever wondered about what happened before your birth? Or about what will happen after death?
5. Have you wondered about the beginning of the world? Or about what will happen at the end of the world?
6. Would it make any difference to you if you found out what happened in the beginning of the world and what will happen at the end of the world?

animal, vegetable or mineral 'thing' or 'word' or 'thought' in the challenger's head – but always be ready to change your mind in the light of the responses you get.

So 'Twenty Questions' teaches the lesson that scientists very quickly find out. 'Twenty Questions' can also illustrate what happens when the chain of questioning goes badly wrong. While there are many examples in the history of scientific breakthroughs of scientists discovering questions waiting to be answered, there are also many more examples of scientists asking the wrong questions. Often our best response is to ask a good question.

QUESTIONS IN RELIGION AND SCIENCE

Every January, a big science festival for second-level students, the Young Scientist Exhibition, is held in the Royal Dublin Society, Ballsbridge, Dublin. It is amazing to go around the exhibits and see the variety of questions that these young researchers have been working with for months. They are curious and confident, and the scientific age has encouraged them. Questions in the last few years include: How can we know that food has gone too bad to eat? Are there new techniques to solve mathematical equations? What are the intervals between prime numbers? How is Europe being urbanised?

If, by contrast, you visit many Religious Education classes up and down the country, you may hear another set of questions, no less interesting, such as: how can we know that God exists? What do we know about Jesus? Is the Bible authentic? Is the story of creation in the book of Genesis really true? How does a miracle work?

For discussion

1. Sometimes people have the experience of asking the wrong question. Did you ever have this experience? What did you learn?
2. Interviewers on radio and television have to be expert questioners. Discuss the art of interviewing with someone in the media, and find out how such a person approaches the task of questioning.
3. Scientists and researchers tell us that finding the right question is the real problem, not finding the answer. Did you or any of your friends ever try to conduct research (like the Young Scientist Exhibition)? Tell the story of the research and draw lessons about questioning.
4. If you were interviewing somebody who had survived a car-crash or accident of some sort, what questions would you need to ask them to find out the full story?
5. A launderette in Dublin has a notice over its bank of washing machines: 'There are no stupid questions.' What do you think the owner means? Why did he or she put up the notice? Is the statement true?

Assignments

1. Look at a newspaper story and identify the different questions framing the construction of the article. Try to locate where each question is answered.

   It may help you to know that when a journalist writes a story, he or she sometimes answers questions in a certain order: 'What? Where? When? Who? How? Why? What next? So what?' Notice that this order of questions puts the more factual questions first (What? Where? When? Who?) and the matter-of-opinion questions later (How? Why? What next? So what?).

2. Make a list of questions, covering both science and religion, that interest you. Are any of them NOT covered in this section of the Religious Education course?

Resources for further study
See teacher's text on CD-Rom for further suggestions.

This topic is also considered in **Section H, The Bible: Literature and Sacred Text**.

Bertrand Russell

These two sets of questions mirror the questions of scientists and theologians through the ages. In general, a rough guide is that science answers 'how' questions and religion answers 'why' questions. But there are many areas common to both science and religion. Science and religion, for example, have many 'what', 'where', 'when' and 'who' questions.

Big science questions include: How is the material world composed? How can we find new sources of energy? How can we get to a nearby planet? How does the force of gravity work? How are traits passed on from parents to children? How did human life come about?

Big religion questions include: Why do I exist? Why should people be good to one another? Why is the universe beautiful, orderly and intelligible? Why is there evil in the universe? Why is life so unfair? Why bother to search for truth? Why bother to do anything other than survive?

But there are really big questions that cover both science and religion, including questions about beginnings (cosmology and creation) and endings (destiny of the universe and the next life). For instance: how or why did the universe come about? How or why will the universe end? What does that mean for human beings?

OVER-SIMPLIFICATION

It is very easy to over-simplify our answers. We do that usually by ignoring important sides of the question. For both science and religion, over-simplifications are dangerous.

In science, over-simplification is called scientism. **Scientism** claims that science can answer all of our questions. The only reliable knowledge and information is scientific knowledge. 'What science cannot tell us, man cannot know,' as the philosopher Bertrand Russell said. (He meant women as well, of course.)

Fideism is religious over-simplification. **Fideism** means 'faith-ism'. It holds that all we need is religious faith. Fideists believe that reason is unnecessary and, indeed, is an obstacle to gaining true knowledge. A particular kind of fideism is **fundamentalism**. Fundamentalists hold to the Bible (or other religious scriptures) or a statement of religious doctrine as all we need to know.

Evangelist Billy Graham

Grand Ayatollah Fazel Lankarani

Both of these approaches come from presenting science as fact, and religion as faith. In other words, science is supposed to be totally objective, and religion totally subjective. Science is thought to be 'out there', obvious, clearly seen, indisputable, beyond controversy and very certain. Religion is supposed to be 'in your head', 'just your opinion', mental, personal, open to dispute, controversial and quite uncertain.

In this book, we maintain that science is not just fact, but also a point of view, and that religion is not just faith, but also reason and common sense. In other words, scientific facts lead to personal opinions and convictions, and religious opinions ought to include factual evidence.

Revision of Important Terms

Look up the following terms which you have come across in this chapter and briefly explain each one. Each of these terms is printed in bold in the text.

Stereotypes, Scientism, Fideism, Fundamentalism.

For discussion

1. 'Science is fact and religion is opinion.'
2. Think of examples where scientific facts lead to religious opinions, and religious opinions are based on scientific facts.

Assignments

1. Explain the human need to ask questions.
2. Compile and present a list of ultimate questions.
3. Compare and contrast 'scientism' and 'fideism' and show how both do a disservice to their respective disciplines.

In summary...

We have learned that many people rely on stereotypical images of the scientist and the religious person when they think about science and religion. Balance is needed because the educated person today seeks a meaning for life, and society needs answers to pressing environmental, ethical and political problems. We also need to avoid simplistic answers: such as scientism and fundamentalism.

Chapter 2

Community

'There is no such thing as society.'

Margaret Thatcher (UK prime minister 1979-1990)

Resources for further study
See teacher's text on CD-Rom
for further suggestions.

> **In this chapter you will learn about...**
>
> *...the scientific and theological communities. We focus on the idea of community and appreciate how we are all formed by the societies in which we live. We have particular experiences and situations that shape our ideas, and so each of us is really the child of a particular time and place. This is true for scientists and religious people as much as anyone else. Then we study in some detail what scientists and religious people do, as members of different communities of enquiry who interpret their experiences in order to make meaning of their lives.*

This topic is also considered in
**Section A, The Search for
Meaning and Values; Section B,
Christianity: Origins and
Contemporary Expressions** and
Section C, World Religions.

COMMUNITIES OF ENQUIRY

In 1987, the prime minister of the United Kingdom, Margaret Thatcher, gave an interview to *Woman's Own* magazine which became justly famous. At one point, she commented: 'They're casting their problem on society. And, you know, there is no such thing as society.'

'There is no such thing as society.' Thatcher's philosophy was individualistic, that the individual human being is responsible entirely for his or her own actions, with little need for support or reliance upon others. That belief is called **individualism**.

The opposite belief is **collectivism**, which maintains that individuals exist only for the welfare of the people taken as a whole. For collectivism, society is paramount. Margaret Thatcher was vigorously opposing this doctrine.

There is, however, a middle ground. People are by nature relational. This means that a person can really only grow and develop as a person in a community. Belief in **persons in community** is the middle ground between individualism and collectivism.

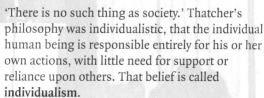

In other words, each of us becomes a person only in the company of others, in our family, in society or in community. We all learn from others to be ourselves. Human thought needs communication with other human beings to be truly human and truly thinking. This is true also for scientific thinking and religious thinking.

'THE WAVE'

In 1967, a teacher in an American high school in California organised a learning experience for his History class. Ron Jones introduced his students to a new movement, called 'The Third Wave'. The movement restricted membership to selected individuals. The new student society became an elite group. Membership was highly regarded, and the other students esteemed the logo and symbols of the society. He wanted the project to teach the emergence of National Socialism (the Nazi Party) in pre-war Germany. Students would understand how ordinary decent people could end up voting for a leader like Adolf Hitler. 'The Third Wave', however, became a serious source of division, and this alarmed Ron Jones. He disbanded the society before it got out of hand. Ron Jones' story was made into a short film called The Wave.

Ron Jones

This illustrates the social power of a group. School students and teenagers take their lead from other young people. One's peers can constitute a **reference group** (the people with whom one compares oneself). Adults also feel the powerful moral pressure of the reference group. We interpret reality and our experience largely from the perspective of the social group to which we belong.

For discussion
Recall your ideas and experience of community/groups when you started in this school. How have your ideas changed in the interim?

Questions
Before answering the questions, make a list of the groups to which you belong, e.g. a sports team, a group of friends, the cast of a play or drama, a prayer or music group, a club or association and so on.
1. Do groups such as these exert an influence on the individual? In what ways?
2. Can you remember such a group that had a good influence on you?
3. Can you remember a group that had a bad influence on you?
4. What did you learn from the different experiences? How were you influenced?
5. In what ways did you change as a result of your membership of such groups?

Assignment
We learn through our community, through the people with whom we associate. Find and read Robert Fulghum's book *All I Really Needed to Know I Learned in Kindergarten*, or at least read the first chapter. Did you have the same experience as Robert Fulghum? What, for example, did you learn from school, from your home, from your neighbourhood or district? Have you noticed differences with other young people who came from other backgrounds, other schools or other districts?

During the Nazi era in Germany, scientists who were unsympathetic with the aims of the National Socialist Party (Nazis) or of non-Aryan origin (for instance, Jews) were expelled or excluded from universities, colleges and research institutes. Robert K. Merton, the American sociologist, remarked that the political party spirit of the Nazis and the ethos of science were incompatible. **Ethos** means the characteristic spirit or atmosphere of any social group, like a school or college, business or organisation, community or association.

For discussion

1. Religion (like politics) is usually personal, involving individual commitment, trusting and accepting. Discuss how scientists and religious people have clearly different attitudes.
2. Are your scientific friends more impersonal, detached, unbiased and sceptical than you? What do you think happens when like-minded people spend a lot of time together and communicate a lot among themselves?

Questions

1. According to Merton, the ethos of science contains what four key elements?
2. Explain each of these elements, giving examples where possible.

Merton described the ethos of science as containing four key elements:

- Science is *impersonal*: a statement should always be tested impersonally, no matter who says it.
- Science is *communal*: discoveries and inventions should be the property of everyone; they belong to the community of scientists through the ages and around the world.
- Science is *detached*: there should be no personal motives and biased considerations in scientific work.
- Science is *sceptical*: all facts should be checked, all conclusions questioned, and all arguments tested.

THE SCIENTIFIC COMMUNITY

'If I have seen farther, it is by standing on the shoulders of giants.' So Isaac Newton claimed in a letter to Robert Hooke in 1676. What do you think Isaac Newton meant by that? Was he an acrobat or had he something else in mind?

Isaac Newton

Isaac Newton was a great scientist. Indeed, he himself was a giant of science, and his phrase *'The shoulders of giants'* is now the classic statement of the dependence of science on teamwork, on the accumulation of knowledge, and on the work of past research. It describes the community nature of the scientific enterprise. Scientists admit that what looks like genius is often just painstaking and detailed attention, building on the results reported by others, piecing together bits of a puzzle collected by colleagues around the world. Success, someone said, is ninety per cent perspiration and ten per cent inspiration!

When a new insight is gained, the scientist communicates it to fellow researchers to seek confirmation, affirmation and, indeed, applause for the discovery. Early publication is the usual way to stake a claim to be the first. One publishes one's work so that scientific contemporaries around the world may recognise, acknowledge and accept the discovery.

'SITTING AND STANDING'

There is an old saying: 'Where you stand depends upon where you sit.' This is a powerful statement. It means that what you think is powerfully affected by what is of advantage to you. We follow our **interests**; that is, the things that concern us, that matter to us, that have consequences for us. We are never totally neutral, never completely unbiased, never absolutely fair to all sides. We cannot be, because we already know which side is best for us. 'We know on what side our bread is buttered.'

Scientists claim that science is value-free, neutral and objective. **Objective** means entirely impartial; the investigation is neutral, detached and value-free. **Subjective** means relying mainly on one's own individual point of view.

Assignment

Research an account of a scientific discovery, e.g. *The Sleepwalkers* by Arthur Koestler. Appreciate how scientists profit from the work of predecessors, sometimes see things that the original research missed, and are ordinary, jealous and competitive human beings under the skin!

Science is supposed to be objective. But that is very hard to achieve. For instance, scientists are often engaged in research for military or national or industrial purposes. The Government or industry pays for the research, and millions of euro are involved. The scientists cannot easily bite the hand that feeds them. This means that scientists are influenced by who gives them money. Therefore, it is wise to suspect the claim of scientific objectivity. Scientists are human beings, and human beings have interests.

What Scientists Should Do

(The material from here to the top of page 23 is for Higher Level students only.)

Scientists genuinely hope to be objective, as far as they can. Scientists encourage other scientists to repeat their experiments, duplicate their observations, check their data and see for themselves what they have discovered. The scientific method tries to eliminate the personal and particular, and, at very least, involve a wide variety of observers and experimental conditions during the investigation. Where it is possible, scientists want to rely on the measurable and countable, or, in the best situation, the **empirical** (based on experiment and observation as opposed to ideas based on theory only).

Resources for further study
See teacher's text on CD-Rom for
further suggestions.

Thus, the **scientific method** involves a sequence of observation, hypothesis, experiment, testing and theory. There are four steps in the scientific method:

- Science begins with **observation**. The scientist records and measures the events he or she sees. These measurements are the data from the observation.

- Then a hypothesis or scientific guess is proposed. The scientist tries to imagine the causes of what has been seen. The **hypothesis** is a suggested explanation to account for the data.

- Then the scientist tests the hypothesis by experiment. An **experiment** is an arranged test to check the hypothesis to see if it accords with observable facts. A hypothesis that does not pass the experiment is rejected. A hypothesis that is not falsified (seen to be wrong) is accepted.

- Finally, a hypothesis that survives many experiments and repeated testing is called a theory. A **theory** is a widely accepted hypothesis, which scientists find to be useful, explanatory and, generally speaking, certain.

WHAT SCIENTISTS REALLY DO

This is what scientists are supposed to do. In practice, of course, things are untidy.

A significant stipulation of scientific method is that observation comes before hypothesis. The scientist is supposed to observe neutrally and without an agenda, and then to propose a hypothesis for what he or she observes.

In practice, this often does not happen. Observations are frequently accompanied by an agenda. 'Seeing is a theory-laden undertaking.' (Hansen) The scientist purposely sets out to look for something. He or she has an idea in mind before beginning. Rather than the hypothesis following from observation, the hypothesis is driving the observation.

A second difference between the scientific method and scientific practice concerns the social context. The scientific method should be a process that is impersonal, accountable and transparent, one that could be done again, anywhere and by anyone. It should be blind and impartial.

Question

Is scientific enquiry always objective? (Higher Level)

Assignment

Write a note on the scientific method. (Higher Level)

But the reality is different. All scientific activity takes place in a community of science. Universities depend on scientific research to attract funding. Scientists know which scientific areas will better repay exploration, and lead to greater rewards. There are high-paying areas of all branches of science, and people with money tell scientists which areas they are. Scientists also serve as mentors, referees, evaluators, editors and collaborators to one another. This means that the scientific community makes its own standards and rules. The scientific community approves of what it regards as genuine science.

A third difference from the classic picture of the scientific method lies in the way progress occurs. One would get the idea that science advances by degrees. This is sometimes not the case.

The history of science shows that sometimes scientists change their ideas not bit by bit, so to speak, but at 'one fell swoop' in a huge upset of thinking. Great change comes not by many small steps, but by large jumps.

'That's one small step for man, one giant leap for mankind.'

Neil Armstrong, the Apollo astronaut and the first man on the moon, famously said when he stepped on to the lunar surface: 'That's one small step for man, one giant leap for mankind.' He could say it, because he was the first one there.

Resources for further study
See teacher's text on CD-Rom for further suggestions.

A minor adjustment can cause a huge change in our point of view. Science has seen enormous shifts of perspective throughout history, which were revolutionary at the time, and yet depended on seemingly insignificant details.

The phrase **paradigm shift**, invented by Thomas Kuhn, describes the process. According to Kuhn, a **paradigm** is a framework of ideas comprehensively explaining a field of study. It is like scaffolding on the front of a tall building. While a particular paradigm is thought to be true, science proceeds 'normally', in general following the classic scientific method. The scientists all scramble up using the scaffolding,

Thomas Kuhn

sure that the platforms and structure can bear the weight of their thought. But when the paradigm begins to wobble, it often happens that the old framework comes crashing down in ruins. And then a new framework may suddenly emerge, and the shift from one set of supports to the other may be astonishingly quick.

The move from the medieval world-view to the science of Copernicus was one example of a paradigm shift. Other examples include the three revolutions of ideas in the late nineteenth and early twentieth centuries: Darwin's evolutionary theory, Freud's theory of the unconscious, and Einstein's theory of relativity. These massive shifts in scientific thought and general culture make up much of the story of science's challenge to religion.

(End of Higher Level material)

THE THEOLOGICAL COMMUNITY

Church Life

Every Saturday and Sunday, our television schedules are filled with programmes about football. Hours are consumed with live broadcasts, studio discussions, 'build-up', 'analysis', replays, and then 'Match of the Day'. Have you ever wondered how many people actually go to a professional football game in England, Scotland, Wales or Ireland each weekend? Would you say that more people go to football than go to church each weekend? Think about that for a minute.

Actually, more people go to church. This is, of course, not to say that people are more interested in religion than in football, nor that more young people go to church than go to football games. Just that, as a matter of fact, more people pass through the doors of churches, chapels and meeting houses up and down the country, than attend professional football games on any given weekend.

This action by such a large number of people, making time and taking the trouble to come together every week for an hour or so, has an immense impact on our common culture. Religious ideas run very deep in our hearts. Many of us turn to religion in our moments of great joy and great sorrow. Births, marriages and deaths, crises in personal life, setbacks and failures, all of these often drive us back to our religious roots.

For discussion

Ask relatives or older friends about the feelings they had when Neil Armstrong walked on the moon for the first time in July 1969, or when they heard of the first heart transplant by Christian Barnard in 1967, or when they heard of the first atomic bomb explosion in 1945. Did they think that the world had changed? Did they feel differently about things? Did they expect that everything would be the same afterwards?

This topic is also considered in **Section A, The Search for Meaning and Values** and **Section G, Worship, Prayer and Ritual**.

For discussion

Have you any examples of the impact of religious ideas on our culture, for example the impact of Christianity on Irish society? What positive or negative effects do these have?

GRADUATION CEREMONIES

Do you have a Graduation Service or Mass at your school? Have you ever been at a Graduation Ceremony in a college or university? Could you describe what happens?

Ceremonies like graduations involve a few different things: usually a procession or parade, special costumes or garments, like academic gowns or hats, a parchment or document or medal or memento of the occasion. Each graduate walks up individually to the stage for a presentation from the President. The word 'graduation' comes from the Latin for 'step'. Stepping up is a very meaningful exercise for the graduate. It symbolises that the student is taking a step, leaving the student level and completing an important stage of education.

RITUAL AND CEREMONY

Ceremonies and rituals survive through the generations. They play a major role in all religions. Ceremonies and rituals embody traditions and attitudes that last a long time and are shared by a large number of people. Every time a ceremony or ritual is enacted, people remind themselves of the values and feelings that underlie it. Once again, they participate in an emotional and spiritual community that unifies people in a particularly powerful way.

A **ritual** is a stable pattern of activity, something we do in the same way every time we do it. It could be a trivial, thoughtless action, like shaking hands, or clapping someone in applause, or something more thoughtful, like sending someone a birthday card, or bringing a bouquet of flowers to someone who is sick.

A **ceremony** is an extended and elaborate ritual, built around a significant human event, such as birth, death, marriage, or rite of passage, like the transition to adulthood, graduation and so on. It is not a passing gesture or casual formality. A ceremony sums up and intensifies the thoughts and emotions of the group at a special occasion, in order to remember the past, strengthen the present and determine the future.

1. When have you felt moved, emotional, uplifted and excited by a ceremony, either in church or elsewhere?
2. Did you feel 'one' with the other people present? How did the unity show itself?
3. Which values were being celebrated and sustained in that ritual?

Religious ceremony creates community. A religion is called a 'community of meaning' because it helps people to interpret what happens to them and it gives them a sense of certainty, purpose, direction and motivation as they encounter the ups and downs of life.

First-Order Activity and Second-Order Activity

Some things, you just do. You jump out of a plane with a parachute strapped to your back – your first skydive. The wind hits you and drives the breath out of you. As you stick out your arms and flatten yourself out like a hovering eagle, the air seems to pick you up, and the sensation of falling completely disappears. You can even move yourself sideways, almost as you would in the water, swimming in the atmosphere, and the feeling is intoxicating. You have never enjoyed anything so much before. Even conscious that you are hurtling towards a hard landing below, hoping at the back of your head that nothing goes wrong with the parachute when you finally pull the ripcord, you are exhilarated. You are on a high... Skydiving is a first-order activity. Like Nike, just do it.

Other things, you think about afterwards. Back on good old mother earth, you think about your experience. How did that happen? What was going on as you sliced through the air, gliding effortlessly through space? As you came down, circling closer and closer to the surface, you were conscious as never before of the eddies and whirls of air, of the drift of the prevailing wind, of the gusts that took you up momentarily and bore you aloft. Your curiosity might be aroused. You might enquire about the science of flight, study aeronautics, find out something about meteorology and weather, examine the way birds do it and so on. Thinking about the experience, and relating it to existing knowledge, is a second-order activity, an activity of thinking about the experience.

WHAT DOES THEOLOGY DO?

(The material from here to the end of the chapter is for Higher Level students only.)

Religious experiences are similar. We experience our relationship with God and with other people directly. We pray. We worship. We act morally and responsibly. We sin. We have a sense of failure. We are forgiven. We sense a gift of grace. We know in our hearts that life is meaningful. We believe that God is responsible for our lives and our world. We hope in the future. We love God and our neighbour.

Assignment

Explain, with examples, first-order activity and second-order activity.

Pilgrims at the Wailing Wall, Jerusalem

Resources for further study
See teacher's text on CD-Rom for further suggestions.

When we ask questions, think critically about and reflect upon our religious experience, we are 'doing theology'. The study of God belongs to the discipline called **theology** (Greek *theos* meaning 'god' and *logos* meaning 'word' or 'talk').

Theology helps us to sort out our experiences and our ideas about God, about human beings, about the relationship between them, about destiny, about the world and about history. Theology asks the hard questions:

How do you know that? What do you mean by that?
Is what you are saying credible?
Is what you are saying coherent?
Where do we go from here?

WHO IS GOD FOR YOU?

This topic is also considered in Section A, The Search for Meaning and Values; Section B, Christianity: Origins and Contemporary Expressions and Section C, World Religions.

A thinker once said: 'Tell me who your God is, and I will tell you whether I believe in him or not.' He was making the point that the question of God's existence and nature is not a straightforward issue, when compared to a scientific question, like finding out whether life exists on Mars.

Ask people about their concept of God, and you will come across very different ideas. Some have a vague notion that there is a 'force behind it all'. Others think of a wise old man in the sky, or maybe a cosmic mind, or they may deny that there is any God at all.

Questions

1. What do you understand by 'doing theology'?
2. Who is God for you? (Higher Level)

Assignment

Can you begin to 'unpack these words' for yourself: God, Human, Love, Being? (Higher Level)

Some words contain a lot of meaning. 'God' is one such word. 'Human' is another. A third is 'love'. A fourth word that is jam-packed full of meaning is 'being'. All of these words are very short, but the moment that you try to lay out what is contained in them, you find that they hold an enormous amount of significance. The 1960s came up with a marvellous phrase to describe what we do when we try to clarify meaning: we have to 'unpack these words'.

We need to 'unpack' the content of God, who is the object of theology. We have an immediate difficulty in that God is not a thing or a material object and so is not what science studies. God is not open for inspection by observation or experiment. Our language is fine for describing things in the material world but it is very inadequate when speaking of the infinite God.

TWO KINDS OF THEOLOGY

Theology has taken two ways to find out about God: natural theology and revealed theology. First human beings tried to find out about God using only our own resources. **Natural theology** tries to obtain knowledge of the existence of God by the use of reason alone. Thomas Aquinas's Five Ways of proving God's existence is the classic example of natural theology. If God created the universe, then we can discover something about God from creation. We know about God by looking at God's works. But looking at what God has made does not tell us a lot about God's self.

To find out about God, we need to hear from God. God has to contact us and talk to us in some way. In **revealed theology**, God tells us about God's self. The Christian understanding of God is based on the Bible, the word of God, the record of God's self-revelation. Christians believe that God reveals, above all, in Jesus Christ, whose story is told in the four gospels of the New Testament.

'Revelations' by Albrecht Dürer

THE COMMUNITY OF CHRISTIAN FAITH

God's revelation is passed on from human being to human being; this is called the Christian tradition. Just as scientists share their findings, check each other's work, verify each other's results, learn from each other's research, so Christians will look at the views of God that others have experienced, in other countries and in other centuries, and make them their own. All the different experiences of God, throughout the ages, and all the different words of God, to different people, are shared and treasured by those who listen to God's word and appreciate God's work.

The Christian Church is the community of people founded by Jesus Christ who share their faith in him and who are challenged to follow him in their lives. Theology, natural and

revealed, is a communal activity because it studies the shared faith of the Christian community. It tries to give an account of God's revelation to the original community of faith in biblical times, how it passed on in the tradition, and how it relates to us today.

EVER CHANGING, EVER THE SAME

This means that theologians, too, are men and women of their time. If God has to speak to human beings in human language, then human language is used for theological ideas. Furthermore, if the language changes, theological understanding will also change. An explanation that would make perfect sense in one culture will be deficient when translated into another. This is because an explanation makes sense only when it is directed to the understanding and knowledge of a particular audience. If the audience is different, the explanation also should be different.

Religious faith, however, in the end, is based on the conviction that God is active in human history, and that human beings can encounter God. There is only one God. Religious faith is clear that God is the foundation for all that exists, the unchanging force for creativity in the universe, and the eternal relationship that personally accompanies each human being through life. This means that there is a unity of theme in theology that binds together different approaches or traditions. The word 'religion' means to bind together, and the theology that represents the understanding and expression of the religious experience of a faith, and indeed of all the world's faith communities, exhibits somewhat of a common perspective across cultures and civilisations and centuries.

Questions

1. Differentiate between natural theology and revealed theology.
2. How is theology a 'communal activity'? (Higher Level)

Assignments

1. How would you define community? Outline the reasons for the importance of community in theology and science.
2. Write a note on the theological method and the theories of interpretation available to theology. (Higher Level)

Revision of Important Terms

Look up the following terms which you have come across in this chapter and briefly explain each one. Each of these terms is printed in bold in the text.

Individualism, Collectivism, Persons in community, Reference group, Ethos, Interests, Objective, Subjective, Empirical, Scientific method, Observation, Hypothesis, Experiment, Theory, Paradigm, Paradigm shift, Ritual, Ceremony, Theology, Natural Theology and Revealed Theology.

In summary...

In this chapter, we realised the importance of community in forming ideas and attitudes, whether they are scientific or religious. Community is necessary for human progress and personal insight and growth.

We distinguished between objective and subjective investigation in science, and noted that complete objectivity is almost impossible to achieve.

We traced the scientific method in its stages, and saw how the scientific and academic community can affect it.

We then turned to religious life, especially in the community called Church, and noted the difference between first- and second-order activity. Theology is the reflective second-order analysis of religious life and thought. There are two kinds of theology: natural theology and revealed theology, and these make up two different interpretations of religious experience.

Part 2: The Relationship between
Religion and Science

Chapter 3

Ancient and Medieval Perspectives on Religion and Science

'What is the stars?'

Captain Boyle, *Juno and the Paycock*

In this chapter you will learn about...

...*what people thought about the world before the advent of modern science. We begin with our own astronomical observations, through which we hope to journey back into the minds of scientists more than eight hundred years ago. Then we can understand how they believed the world and the sky were constructed. The ideas of Ptolemy, Aristotle and St Thomas Aquinas will be explored to enable us to present a portrait of the world from which Galileo's ideas emerged. So we will appreciate the innovations of Nicolas Copernicus, who first seriously proposed that the sun travelled around the earth. Galileo's methods and contribution will be discussed in Chapter 4.*

Resources for further study
See teacher's text on CD-Rom for further suggestions.

ANCIENT ASTRONOMY

'An' as it blowed an' blowed, I often looked up at the sky, an' assed meself the question, What is the stars, what is the stars?' The character Captain Boyle in Seán O'Casey's play *Juno and the Paycock*, shares his deep philosophical search with his drinking partner and fellow waster, Joxer Daley. 'What is the stars?' So, like Captain Boyle, let us spend some time looking up at a clear starry night. There are about two thousand stars visible to the naked eye at any one time.

If you watch for a number of nights, you will notice that almost all of the

This topic is also considered in **Section A, The Search for Meaning and Values**.

points of light do not move in relation to one another. They are in the same position relative to one another night after night. Because the stars do not seem to move in relation to one another, they are called **'fixed stars'**.

For hundreds and thousands of years, the stars have spread the same patterns across our night sky. These patterns are called **constellations**, which means 'grouped stars'. And because the patterns were seen to resemble people or animals or objects, the ancients gave them names, like the Archer, or the Lion, or the Twins and so on. These labels have survived through thousands of years because they make a convenient map of the fixed stars.

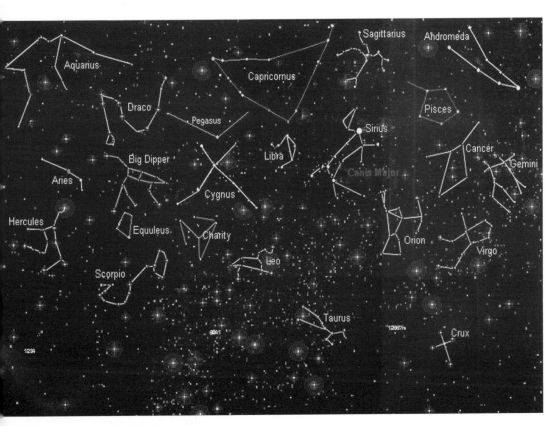

The stars do not move *in relation to one another*. They do, however, move across the sky, from dusk to dawn, in an unending procession of constellations. They rise in the East, cross the roof of the heavens, and set in the West, in the same way that the sun journeys across the daytime sky.

WHAT IS THE MOON?

Captain Boyle and Joxer Daley continued to speculate about life and the universe. 'What is the moon?' the Captain enquires, and Joxer pronounces 'That is the question'.

The moon rises in the East and passes across the sky to the West, like the rest of the stars. But it moves among the fixed stars. You will see it going among the constellations, going from one to the other, as time passes. Actually, if you could watch the moon over an extended period, you would notice that, in the course of the year, it passes through twelve of them. These make up its yearly journey or path. You know the twelve constellations visited by the moon as the **signs of the zodiac**, or the **horoscope.**

Can you identify some of the signs of the zodiac in the night sky, and point them out to your friends? Their names are Pisces, Aquarius, Capricorn, Sagittarius, Scorpio, Libra, Virgo, Leo, Cancer, Gemini, Taurus and Aries.

The second thing you notice about the moon, if you watch it over the period of a few weeks, is that it seems to

Signs of the Zodiac carvings in Amiens Cathedral, France

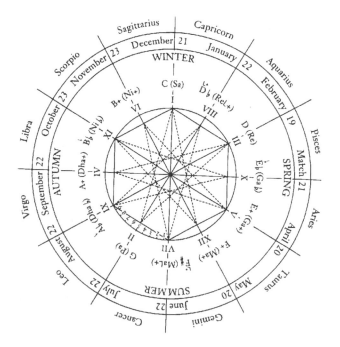

For discussion

What do you understand by the signs of the zodiac? In what ways are people influenced by their horoscopes?

change shape. Sometimes it is a round, fully lit disc like a coin. Sometimes it is a narrow banana or crescent shape. In the course of four weeks, it changes from being quite invisible (new moon) to a round pie in the sky (full moon), passing through partial crescents along the way. These are called the **phases of the moon**, and we time our year by the four times seven days it takes the moon to go through all of its changes. This period of time, of twenty-eight or so days, is called the

month, of course (notice the 'moon' in the 'month'). The seven days of a moon phase is our week.

WANDERING STARS

The ancient observers of the sky soon noticed other travellers across the night sky that followed the path of the zodiac. As these were not fixed stars, they called them **planets**, from the Greek word for 'wanderer'. Just like the moon, a planet passes through the twelve zodiac constellations in a year. The ancient astronomers identified five such planets: Mercury, Venus, Mars, Jupiter and Saturn.

Can you find a planet or two? Well, you could now try to identify them. We cannot give you any precise instructions for finding the planets because we do not know when you will begin looking. You will need to consult the newspapers or ask someone who is interested in astronomy. Or you could consult astronomy websites on the Internet. Some of them have instructions for viewing the night sky each month.

You will be able to distinguish a planet from the surrounding stars because it is quite bright compared to most of the stars, and it moves through the constellations night by night, and it does not twinkle. (Only stars twinkle!)

The one planet we may be able to help you to locate, however, is Venus, or the Evening Star. It is so called because often it is visible at sunset in the South or South-West, about half-way up the sky, very bright, and clearly visible, even while the red sunlight of the setting sun is still flooding the landscape. This is because Venus is quite close to the sun, the second planet away, and nearer to the sun than Earth. Venus is very beautiful and impressive too, as it seems to usher in the night sky, gently covering the earth with darkness.

Mars, Jupiter and Saturn may be found anywhere in the general path of the sun and moon across the sky. Jupiter and Saturn are very big planets and so are quite bright and clear. Mars is slightly smaller and dimmer, but has a distinctive reddish shade.

THE ANCIENT SCIENTIST

The ancient scientists watched the skies with great persistence and precision, and, of course, if they lived in the Middle East or Mediterranean countries, they would have had better weather than you have!

Ancient scientists and scholars realised that the world was round and that we did not live on a flat earth. How do you think they knew that the world was round?

Here are some of the things the ancient scientists noticed:

- Ships seemed to come out of the sea when approaching the shore, suggesting that the surface of the ocean is rounded, and it always was rounded too.

- If you climbed a mountain or a very high tower, you could see more of the surrounding countryside, again suggesting that the surface of the earth is rounded.

- When the world came between the sun and the moon, a shadow of the earth seemed to fall on the moon, and it was rounded too.

- Constellations and planets which set in the West, appear again in the Eastern sky after a regular interval, presumably as they pass below (or around) the earth.

Group work

Forget everything you ever learned about geography or the science of the world and sky. Suppose you knew only what you could see with your naked eye. What would you think about the universe? Take some time to discuss with your friends how you would describe and picture the universe.

Questions

1. Distinguish between stars, constellations and planets.
2. How do the 'phases of the moon' impact on our lives?

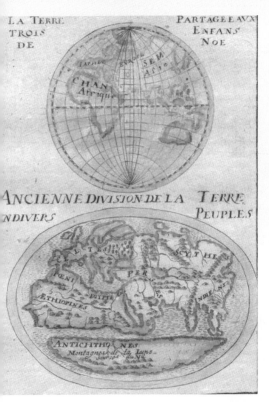

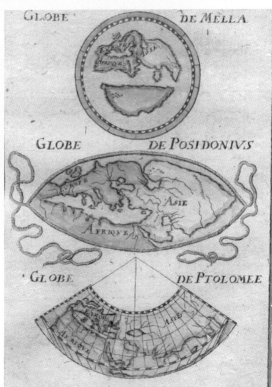

Resources for further study
See teacher's text on CD-Rom for further suggestions.

Now at least, you know the roundness of the earth from your own observations, rather than just believing it on the word of other people.

Is the earth moving or not? The ancient scientists thought the earth was immobile. Why did they think that?

Here are some of the things they noticed:

- The pattern of the stars does not change through the year. The stars look the same no matter what time of the year it is. The stars should seem to shift position if the earth were moving. As the stars stay exactly the same, astronomers concluded that the earth does not move.

Assignment
Write a note about: (1) how the ancient scientists and scholars realised that the world was round, and (2) why the ancient scientists thought the earth was immobile.

- The sun looks as if it moves. The earth feels as if it does not.

- If the earth moved, things on the surface of the earth would be flung off.

- If the earth moved, an arrow shot straight up into the air would land somewhere else, because the ground beneath would have shifted while it was flying up and down.

Hence the ancient scientists concluded that the earth is round and immobile, and that the sun and moon and stars and planets travel around it.

PTOLEMY

PTOLEMY'S UNIVERSE

How did the ancient scientists explain the movement of the stars and the planets, the sun and the moon?

Ptolemy, an ancient astronomer who lived around 150 CE, said that there was a huge transparent sphere which held the stars, along with seven more spheres, one each for the five planets, the moon and the sun. He maintained that each of them turned independently, with the round earth as centre. The moon's sphere was the nearest, then the one for Mercury, and then the one for the sun and the other planets in the order of Venus, Mars, Jupiter and Saturn. Finally, the sphere carrying the stars across the sky turns on the outside. **Ptolemy's system of the universe** is depicted in our illustration. It was the common scientific explanation of the planets and stars for over a thousand years.

Ptolemy c. 100-178 CE

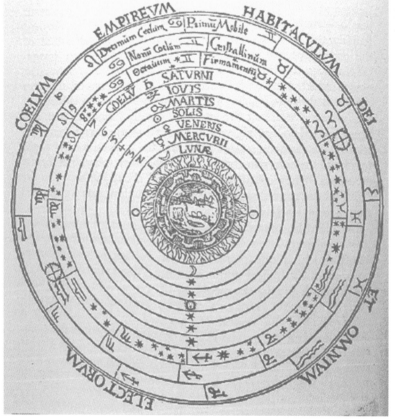

Ptolemy's system of the universe

When the ancient scientists closely examined the movement of the planets, however, they had problems. Each planet varies in brightness, suggesting that it may be further away from the earth at some times than at others. In addition, each planet at times appears to go backwards, which would detach it from its transparent sphere. How do you think the scientists two thousand years ago solved these problems?

They imagined that each planet was attached to a smaller circle which whirled around on the bigger sphere, so at times it appeared to go backwards as well as forwards. If you think of a ferris wheel, with the chairs swinging back and forth, and sometimes, maybe, swinging right up and around, you will have an idea of what the ancient astronomers thought was happening with the planets.

'SAVING THE APPEARANCES'

You might have noticed that we used a very careful phrase in the last paragraph. We said that 'each planet...appears to go backwards'. The reason for the word 'appears' is very interesting. You could ask 'Is the planet *really* going backwards?' or you could ask 'Are you saying that the planet *seems* to be going backwards?'

The answer to these questions goes to the heart of scientific thinking. The problem is whether the explanation is meant to describe what *actually* exists or whether it is meant to be a help to *predict* what we are investigating. In other words, is the theory *true* or is it just *useful*?

Assignment

Describe briefly Ptolemy's system of the universe.

Many ancient scientists knew that the crystal spheres might not exist in reality. Ptolemy's system, for example, included forty spheres. That was a very complicated contraption indeed, and difficult to imagine really existing. But that did not matter because they could do their calculations about speeds and directions, and predict an eclipse or the appearance of a planet, using Ptolemy's system. What mattered was the ability to predict the future. Ptolemy's system was a sufficient explanation for what seemed to be happening, or, as they said, it was **'saving the appearances'**.

THE MEDIEVAL WORLD-VIEW

THE MEDIEVAL WORLD-VIEW

Imagine that you are an educated person in the Middle Ages, around 1100 or 1200 CE, and that you know all of this and are very familiar with Ptolemy's system of the universe. Now how does that make you feel? What do you think about the universe, about the place of the earth, about human beings, about nature? Do you think that the universe is big or small? Do you feel comfortable or hopeful about the future of the human race? Do you think that the universe is a friendly or frightening place?

The first thing that can be said is that you know that the universe is finite, that it has boundaries and it comes to an end. So far as medieval scientists can see, and do not forget that they have no telescopes, the universe is quite small.

You also know that the earth does not move, that it is at the centre of the universe, and that all the other planets and stars move around it. Everything moves to its natural place, which for material things is down to earth, and for non-material things is up to the heavens. Earth will always stay below everything else, but Water will be above it. Then there is Air, and over the Air will be Fire. So, Fire and heat rise while Water and rain fall.

Above the moon, in the heavens, there is perfection. There is no Earth, Air, Fire or Water. Planets and stars move in perfect

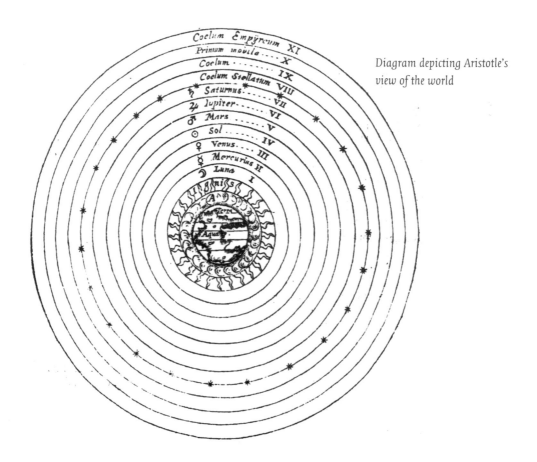

Diagram depicting Aristotle's view of the world

circles as their natural motion. Under the moon, things move in straight lines if pushed, but, if left alone, they will naturally come to their natural rest. So stability is the usual state for all things on earth. This means that things stay where they are put and do not move unless shifted by other things.

Finally, you know that humans are the most important beings in the whole universe (apart from God) and that, in a way, everything revolves around them. This makes you feel very comfortable, as if it was entirely natural that the sun rises and sets – especially for the benefit of the human race. You know that the ancient scientists have carefully investigated all these questions, and that the answers are settled and generally agreed for a very long time.

ARISTOTLE (384-322 BCE)

The ancient philosopher Aristotle was responsible for many of these answers. He lived in Greece about three hundred years before Jesus Christ. A bit of a scientist himself, he believed in precise observation and careful thought about the nature of things. He always tried to find the 'causes', or the reasons for things. Aristotle found that there were four kinds of cause: the material cause, the formal cause, the efficient cause and the final cause. True science had to find all the causes. Here is an example to illustrate the four causes.

Let's pretend that you and a group of your pals decide to build a pool table, maybe for your youth club, or for you and your friends in one of your houses. The first thing you do is that you buy some wood, and slate, and netting, and carpentry tools with which to make your table. That is the **material cause**, the stuff that makes up the thing.

This topic is also considered in **Section A, The Search for Meaning and Values** and **Section B, Christianity: Origins and Contemporary Expressions**.

Resources for further study
See teacher's text on CD-Rom for further suggestions.

Then you say 'What should our pool table look like? How big should it be? How high? How long? How many pockets?' Someone gets a plan of a pool table, maybe a blueprint off the Internet, for example, so you have a design of a pool table. That is the **formal cause**, or the idea for the thing.

Now you need someone who can put the materials together. You need a carpenter or a do-it-yourself expert, and one is available and gets to work. She (or he) is the **efficient cause**, who makes something happen.

Now it gets interesting. Another friend arrives in the middle of the hammering and sawing and all the making of the pool table, and says 'What are you doing?' And being completely absorbed with the work, you answer, 'Wait till we're finished!' What you mean is, when you see the finished product, you will understand what it is we were doing. More importantly than that, you will know why we want to do it. You will know that we want to enjoy ourselves playing pool.

This is the **final cause**. Without it, we would not even begin to build a pool table. And so it is, in one way, the first cause, because it is the first thing we think about. And it is also the last cause, because it is the last thing that you will actually need. It is the beginning and the end. The final cause is the purpose of the action. It is called the final cause, because the Latin word *finis* (the same root word as finish) means goal or end or purpose.

Questions

1. Can you make up another example to explain the four causes, say, to a younger brother or sister?
2. True science had to find all the four causes, Aristotle would have believed. Would a modern scientist believe the same?

For discussion

'God has a purpose for everything under heaven.'

Question

What was the *Summa Theologica*?

St Thomas Aquinas (1225-1274 CE)

One medieval thinker who was really excited about Aristotle's philosophy was Thomas Aquinas. Thomas harmonised the reasoning of Aristotle with the teaching of the Catholic Church and the Bible in a grand summary of theology called the *Summa Theologica*. This united what we know about God, the redemption of humanity and God's presence in the Church with what we know about the universe from philosophy and science. This is the reason for the way our medieval person thinks about the universe.

Everything in the universe is a creature, a product of God's creation, and God loves human beings and has placed them here in the middle of the universe for their salvation and God's glory. Animals and plants and the physical world are here to be used, and angels and other spirits guard us and take care of us. Here, below the moon, there is a mixture of perfection and imperfection, and this is where human beings are tested and tempted. But the whole of creation is as it should be, nothing is happening by chance, and God alone knows how or when everything will work out. God has a purpose for everything under heaven.

The Great Chain of Being

The medieval world-view was called **'The Great Chain of Being'**. This was a ladder of beings from the lowest to the highest, from inanimate things, up to God, the creator of all. In this universe, everything had its natural place. The lowest were minerals and rocks, then plants and vegetation, then animals of all kinds, then human beings, who were thought of as a combination of matter and spirit. Above, there were angels, who were pure spirit, and finally God, at the top of creation's ladder and the Final Cause of it all.

The medieval period in Europe was a time of religious faith, expressed in art, music, drama and the liturgy of the Church. The most tangible monuments to Christian thought in the

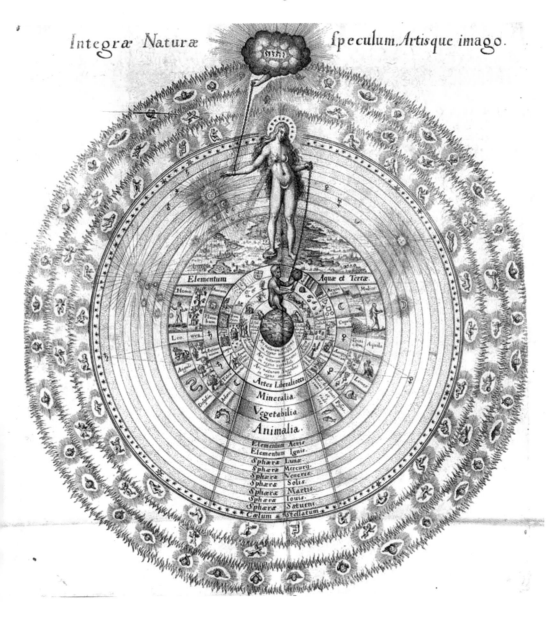

society of medieval Europe were the great cathedrals, dominating the landscape, with spires and towers pointing to heaven in worship. But other towers around Europe were also being directed to the skies, and the men within them were beginning to ask questions that would shake the ground and send the earth itself off on a mad career through infinite space.

COPERNICUS

NICOLAS COPERNICUS (1473-1543 CE)

One of those towers was on the Baltic coast in Poland, occupied by Nicolas Copernicus, forever remembered for starting the earthquake in astronomy. He was a most unlikely 'revolutionary'. He had spent the seventy years of his life as a canon of the cathedral in Frauenburg, a cleric but not a priest. Trained as a doctor and canon lawyer, he had practised medicine, dabbled in finance, and had been, on one occasion at least, a candidate for bishop. But he had a life-long interest that he indulged by looking out from the balcony of his Baltic tower: he was a keen and thoughtful astronomer.

As a student in the University of Krakow and later in Italy, Nicolas had learned Greek and had spent time studying Ptolemy and the other Greek astronomers who disagreed with Ptolemy. He concluded that Ptolemy's calculations could be improved and simplified.

Copernicus wrote a new set of calculations, which he circulated privately. They assumed a **heliocentric** universe (sun as centre) rather than a **geocentric** (earth as centre) and **geostatic** (earth immobile) universe. He did not publish them, not because of Church opposition but from fear of scientific ridicule. His new system was superior to Ptolemy's because the mathematics was easier and simpler. Eventually, colleagues persuaded him to publish his famous book *On the Revolutions of the Heavenly Orbs*, and he did so in 1543, the year of his death. He was handed the first printed copy on his deathbed.

THE COPERNICAN SYSTEM

The book's preface explained that the ideas proposed in the text were only a basis for calculation and not intended to represent the absolute truth of the matter. In other words, according to the preface, the Copernican system was meant just to 'save the appearances'. It is a disputed question ever since whether Copernicus himself wrote the preface. The general agreement among scholars is that an editor wrote the preface in order to deflect criticism from the new publication.

Assignment

Write a short essay on 'The Medieval World-view', taking into account the ideas of Aristotle and Thomas Aquinas. Explain how medieval scientists distinguished between the reality and the appearance of the reality.

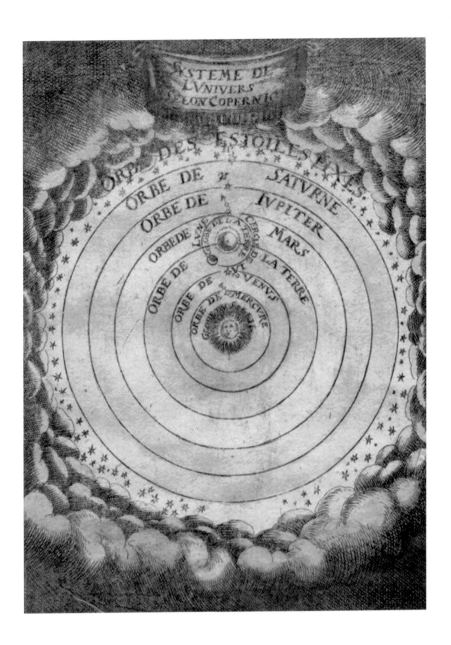

The Copernican system

REACTION TO COPERNICUS

During the next fifty years, reaction to Copernicus' ideas was scanty and scattered.

One reason was that the book was circulated to educated people, mostly scientists and astronomers. It was a complicated volume, written in Latin, and not an easy read. Therefore, Copernicus' arguments travelled slowly. There were no mass media to communicate complicated subjects in simple language for the common people. Copernicus himself said that the book was suitable only for scientists: the title page warned (in Greek): 'Let no one untrained in geometry enter here.'

45

The second reason was that the assumptions in the book were debatable. Copernicus had no direct evidence or proper observations to persuade the scientific community that his assumptions were correct. He had, as we say nowadays, no 'knock-down arguments' to prove his argument. This probably explains his hesitation in publishing the book.

Another reason was that Copernicus was himself carefully conservative, addressing his own preface to the Pope, saying that this was part of the ongoing project of reforming the calendar, on which he had been invited to consult by the Lateran Council.

Questions

1. Why was Copernicus reluctant to publish his findings?
2. Why was the reaction to Copernicus' ideas so muted?

Assignment

Write a note on Nicholas Copernicus and his contribution to astronomy.

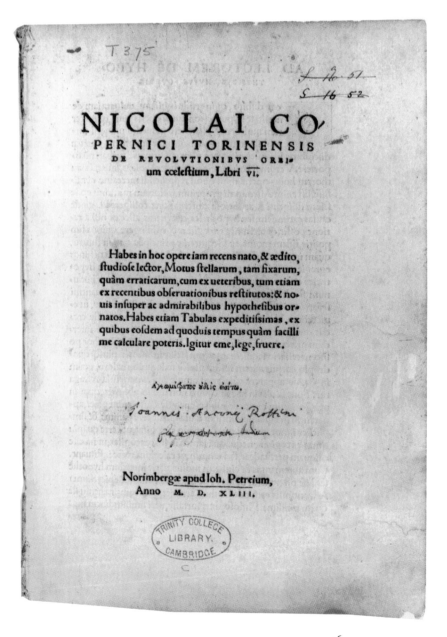

A final reason, in all likelihood, was that the implications of the new way of calculating the movements of the heavenly bodies had yet to be understood, even by Copernicus himself. After all, he had seen nothing new and had, strictly speaking, discovered nothing new. The information with which he worked had essentially been well known for over a thousand years. Copernicus simply approached the information from another direction and succeeded in making more accurate predictions. Thus, the Copernican ideas looked more like a natural development than a revolution. Then someone else would actually see something new...

Revision of Important Terms

Look up the following terms which you have come across in this chapter and briefly explain each one. Each of these terms is printed in bold in the text.

Fixed stars, Constellations, Signs of the zodiac, Horoscope, Phases of the moon, Planets, Ptolemy's system of the universe, 'Saving the appearances', Medieval world-view, Material cause, Formal cause, Efficient cause, Final cause, Great Chain of Being, Copernican system, Heliocentric, Geocentric, Geostatic.

In summary...

We learned how the ancient scientists observed the stars, constellations and planets visible from the surface of the earth. They had no telescopes and were restricted to using only the naked eye. We discovered that they were not ignorant or backward, but were very intelligent in using what they saw to imagine what was happening in the sky and on the earth.

We studied the way that Ptolemy explained the movements of the heavenly bodies. Then we considered the ideas of Aristotle and Thomas Aquinas and, in particular, we distinguished between the reality and the appearance of the reality, recognising that we have two reasons for studying something: to discover the reality, or to predict its behaviour. Finally, we examined the theory of Copernicus and discovered why the people of the Middle Ages found it hard to take on board.

Chapter 4

The Galileo Controversy

'Yet it does move.'

> Saying attributed to Galileo Galilei, after being forced to recant his doctrine that the earth moves around the sun.

In this chapter you will learn...

...to trace the story of Galileo, whose name is connected forever with the most famous controversy in the history of science and religion. We will follow the crisis as it develops from Galileo's observations and conclusions. We will try to assess the principles at stake, describe the various players, look at the way it was resolved at the time, and at how it is judged today.

GALILEO

GALILEO GALILEI (1564-1642 CE)

The one who saw the new things first, and made sure that everyone knew about them, was a redheaded Italian called Galileo Galilei. As a student, he failed to secure a scholarship at the University of Pisa, and left without a degree. His genius was unrecognised then, but that did not last. Seven years later, he was appointed a mathematics teacher at the same university. When he was twenty-six years old, he became professor at the University of Padua. In 1609, Galileo got his hands on a telescope, and never suffered from a lack of recognition since. The first simple telescope (tele = far, scope = see) was constructed in 1608 and it magnified objects seven times. In 1609, Galileo manufactured his own version, which magnified nine times. With his new telescope, he began to examine the heavens.

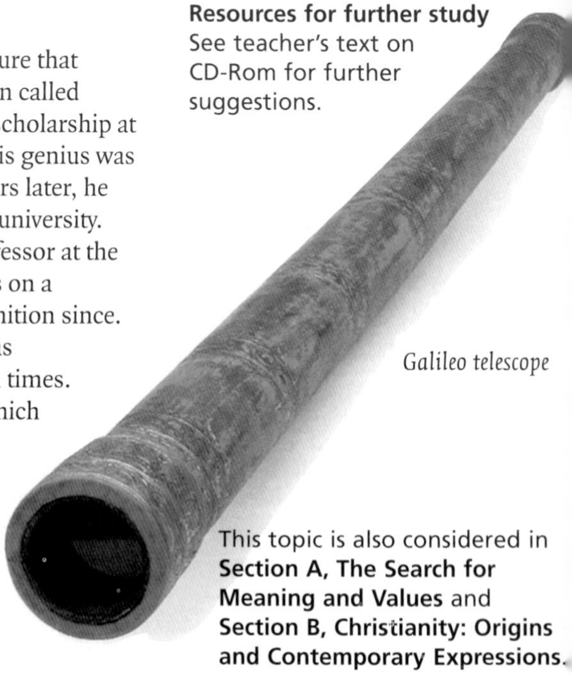

WHAT DID GALILEO SEE FIRST?

Now we come to a **thought experiment.** Galileo was the one who made thought

Resources for further study
See teacher's text on CD-Rom for further suggestions.

Galileo telescope

This topic is also considered in **Section A, The Search for Meaning and Values** and **Section B, Christianity: Origins and Contemporary Expressions.**

experiments famous. He tried to imagine what would happen in different and impossible circumstances in order to see the effect of theory on nature. For instance, what would happen to falling objects which were falling in a vacuum with no earth atmosphere around them? This was impossible to check out in Galileo's time. It could not be done until the astronauts walked on the moon for the first time in July 1969. That night, the world saw on TV for the first time what happens in a perfect space vacuum, and Galileo's imagined ideas were correct.

Let us return to Galileo, looking up into the sky for the first time with his new telescope, trying to hold it steady, with excited heart and nervous hands... What do you think he saw that was really surprising? (If you have a telescope, or binoculars, at home, you can do the experiment yourself, and see what Galileo saw!)

THE SPOTTY GLOBE

The first surprising thing Galileo noticed was that the moon had valleys and mountains. This meant that the moon was not perfect, as the Ptolemaic theory said, but imperfect, like the earth itself. Furthermore, this raised the possibility, even the probability, that the same laws of physics that applied on earth, would apply on the moon as well.

Group work

What do you think he saw? Try to imagine why Galileo would have been so surprised...

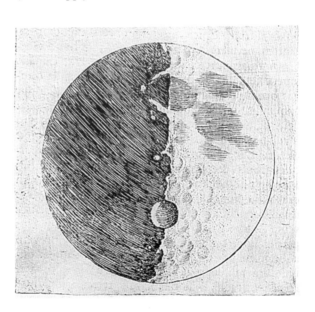

Galileo's own sketch of what he saw through the telescope

John Milton, the great English poet, visited Galileo during a European tour in the year 1633. When he wrote his great epic poem *Paradise Lost*, he made good use of the experience. He described the devil's huge shield by saying that it looked like the moon as Galileo saw it. Milton said that the moon looked like a 'spotty globe'.

Galileo then looked at the sun. (You should never look *directly* at the sun, so Galileo used a piece of paper on which to project an image of the sun from his telescope.) Galileo found spots on the sun as well. Everyone always knew that nothing on earth is perfect, but now it seemed that nothing in heaven is perfect either. The crystal spheres and perfect circles and unchanging flawlessness of the heavens had been clouded.

Another thing that Galileo noticed was that the planets appeared as discs, 'like little moons', and that the stars appeared brighter but not bigger. Galileo could not help noticing that many more stars came into view, as the telescope helped the human eye to see further and further out from earth. This suggested that the stars were further away than scientists had thought.

'Galileo and Milton' by Annibale Gatti

A CRITICAL EXPERIMENT

Galileo was now sure that Ptolemy's system was wrong, that Copernicus was right, that the sun did not go around the earth, that the earth and planets went around the sun, and that only the moon went around the earth. He wanted to settle the question once and for all by a telescopic observation. He was looking for something among the planets that would show changes. This is called a **critical experiment**; that is, a scientific question which, when answered, can resolve a much wider problem. What could Galileo have looked for that would settle the debate?

Galileo thought that Venus – the planet easiest to see – would provide an answer. If Venus showed phases, like the moon does, then the heavens above the moon change, and Ptolemy's system of the universe is wrong. It was clear that the phases of the moon were a result of the sun's rays reflecting from the moon's surface. Something similar on Venus would prove that Venus does not shine by its own light, and that it is part of the changing universe, similar to earth, and surely follows the same scientific laws. Galileo looked at Venus through his new telescope during two months in 1610, and discovered that Venus passes through phases just like the moon.

Galileo wrote what he had discovered in a 1610 booklet called *The Starry Messenger*. It was written in a pithy, factual style and could be described as the first modern scientific report. Galileo reported his observations and described them precisely. In the few months in which he had the new

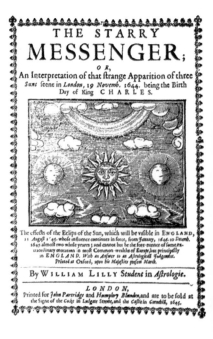

telescope, Galileo made other discoveries too. In particular, he found moons orbiting the planet Jupiter, and he named them, tactfully, after his patron and his relations. We always take care of our sponsors!

Galileo's own sketches of the moons of Jupiter

The impact of The Starry Messenger was immediate. Educated people throughout Europe took notice. They began to understand a number of things: that the planets are similar to the earth, that the universe is much bigger than they had thought and, finally, that the earth is certainly not the centre of everything.

REACTION TO GALILEO

Now here is another 'Thought Experiment'. What did people think about all these new things being discovered? Try to put yourself in the shoes of people who believed in Ptolemy's system of the universe and in the 'Great Chain of Being'. What kind of questions did the new discoveries suggest?

Assignments

1. Write a short biography of Galileo.
2. Explain a 'thought experiment' as made famous by Galileo.
3. What was Galileo's 'critical experiment'?

Here are some of their questions:

- Does the universe contain other inhabited worlds just like this one?

- Where is Heaven?

- And, where might Hell be?

- Then, what about the authority of the Church, of theologians, of the Bible?

- Finally, suppose that the Bible contradicts the scientific account of the universe, saying, for instance, that the earth goes around the sun? Who is to be believed?

THE TWO BOOKS

During the Middle Ages and beyond, thinkers regarded the available knowledge about the universe as contained in **Two Books**: the Book of God's Word (the Sacred Scriptures) and the Book of God's Work (the created universe). One could be read in ancient languages, while the other had to be discerned and discovered from the events and things around us. This was a neat and tidy description of the relationship between natural knowledge and revealed religious doctrine.

It did not help too much, though, if the Two Books seemed to contradict each other. Of course, the believer was clear that the Two Books could not contradict each other. What happened, however, when the scientist suggested that the universe was billions of years old, whereas an examination of the Bible accounts for only about five or six thousand years of history between the moment of creation and now? Maybe the Two Books can contradict each other? Can the truth as discovered by science and as revealed in religion be in conflict?

SCIENCE AND THE BIBLE

These questions about scientific explanations and the interpretation of the Bible lay behind the row that was just beginning to heat up around Galileo. Scientists and theologians were asking how they should read the Two Books of God's Revelation.

We have already learned that there were two ways of understanding scientific explanations or 'reading nature' in the Middle Ages:

Questions

1. What were the 'Two Books' of available knowledge used in the Middle Ages and beyond?
2. Can you think of examples where the Bible seems to contradict scientific teaching?
3. Can you think of examples where religious teaching or moral teaching seems to contradict modern scientific thinking?

This topic is also considered in **Section H, The Bible: Literature and Sacred Text.**

The first was to say that a scientific explanation exactly described what actually existed. (Let us call this principle S 1.)

The second was to say that scientific explanations were calculating tools to help the scientist to predict future events. This was called 'saving the appearances'. (Let us call this principle S 2.)

But there were also a number of ways of interpreting the Sacred Scripture or 'reading the Bible'. Two in particular were discussed at the time of Galileo:

The first was the **literal interpretation of the Bible.** The Bible means exactly what it says. If the statement occurs in Joshua 10:13 that the sun stood still in the middle of the heavens, then that is precisely what happened. (We will call this principle B 1.)

The second was to understand the Bible in an **'accommodated sense'.** The biblical author writes in the language and according to the common understanding of the audience at the time. So, for example, the Bible says that the sun rises in the East and sets in the West, even though we know that the earth goes round the sun, and the movement of the sun is only an appearance. (We will call this interpretation B 2.)

We are now ready to find out what happened to Galileo in the years after his discoveries. Let us take the story in Two Acts.

GALILEO'S FIRST INVESTIGATION

THE GALILEO AFFAIR: 1616

The cast of characters:

GALILEO: redheaded with a real talent for rubbing people the wrong way, sharp of tongue, known to colleagues as 'The Wrangler'; a university professor, politically ignorant, aware of his own intellect, very knowledgeable; interested in everything, incapable of letting things be.

ROBERT BELLARMINE: a Jesuit and cardinal, now over seventy years old, chief theologian of the Catholic Church; taught astronomy when young; highly respected author of a Catechism of Catholic Doctrine; canonised a saint in 1930 and patron of religion teachers.

POPE PAUL V: Camilo Borghese, a canon lawyer in his fifties when he became Pope in 1605; did things legally, inclined to take a hard line on disputes, impatient with new ideas, and personally not in sympathy with people like Galileo.

Group work

Given these four positions, think out the combinations of views that would lead to conflict and that would lead to agreement. Does S 1 with B 1 lead to conflict? What about combining S 2 with B 1? And so on.

Resources for further study
See teacher's text on CD-Rom for further suggestions.

MAFFEO BARBARINI: cardinal and bishop, man of action and politics, well-educated and cultured, admirer of Galileo, self-confident, aware of his own success and concerned with power and influence, a career cleric.

THE STORY SO FAR

At Christmas 1614, a Dominican priest named Caccini preached against Copernican ideas using the text 'Men of Galilee, why stand you looking up to heaven?', punning on Galileo's name. A controversy broke out, especially about the impact of heliocentrism (sun as centre) on biblical interpretation.

Galileo

Bellarmine

Galileo came to Rome to clear the matter up. His friends tried to talk him out of making a fuss, but he persisted. Galileo argued that the Copernican theory was true in fact (S 1) and thus that the Bible should be read in the accommodated sense (B 2).

The Pope formed a Commission to examine the issue of Copernicus' book. Galileo's name was not specifically mentioned. An Irishman, Peter Lombard from Waterford, named Archbishop of Armagh, was on the Commission. Bellarmine and Barbarini were also involved.

What do you think happened? (Take a few minutes to work it out from the characters and the situation. Do not forget the way people were thinking and feeling at the time.)

RESULT OF THE FIRST INVESTIGATION

Pope Paul V

The Commission gave the opinion that the Copernican theory was 'foolish and absurd philosophically and formally heretical' and Copernicus' book

Barbarini

should be suspended until corrected. The first opinion was recorded but not decided. The second was acted on.

By 'philosophically', the experts meant 'scientifically'; and by 'heretical', they meant 'not in agreement with the Bible'. So they favoured the literal interpretation of the Bible (B 1). Galileo's observations had disproved Ptolemy's crystalline spheres, but he could present no proof for the heliocentric theory, and the experts saw that.

Briefly outline the course of Galileo's first investigation from 1614.

Bellarmine advised Galileo to abandon the opinion 'that the sun is the centre of the spheres and immovable and that the earth moves'. He told Galileo to confine himself to the idea that Copernicus 'saved the appearances' (S 2). There was no need for Galileo to get involved with explaining biblical passages, and this would avoid trouble. Interpretation of the Bible was in dispute with the Protestants. Galileo, a layman, would be wise to keep quiet about the Bible.

The rumour spread in Rome that Galileo had been made to renounce his opinion by Bellarmine. Galileo asked Bellarmine for a letter to say that this had not happened. The cardinal signed an official paper, which stated that 'Galileo has not abjured in our hand nor in the hand of anybody else here in Rome'. Galileo's friends had protected him through the tangle of Roman politics. And there, for the moment, the matter rested.

GALILEO'S SECOND INVESTIGATION

THE GALILEO AFFAIR: 1632

The cast of characters:
Within fifteen years, the cast of characters has changed. Robert Bellarmine and Pope Paul V are dead. The other two are older; Galileo himself is approaching seventy years old and, in the meantime, Maffeo Barbarini has been elected Pope and taken the name Urban VIII.

THE STORY A BIT FURTHER ON

When Galileo heard that his friend was now the Pope, he went to see him. During six visits, Urban VIII endorsed Galileo's work in the warmest terms. The Pope would not reverse the 1616 decree, but he agreed that Galileo would write a book explaining the systems of the universe, but without backing any of them. The Pope advised Galileo to 'save the appearances' and suggested a pet idea of his own for the debate.

Galileo wrote the book called *Dialogue on the Great World Systems*. He set it as a debate between Salviati, a well-informed Copernican, Sagredo, an interviewer, and Simplicio, a somewhat slow conservative. Simplicio brings in the pet idea of Urban VIII. Otherwise, the book heavily backed Copernicus.

The book was published in 1632. The Pope was furious. Galileo had betrayed his trust and good will. He concluded that Galileo meant to poke fun at him personally by casting him as Simplicio.

Now, what do you think happened?

ANOTHER INVESTIGATION

The **Inquisition** summoned Galileo to a hearing at the Pope's command. The Inquisition was a tribunal formed to inquire into a denial of Christian doctrine. But everything was conducted very politely and courteously. Galileo was not in any real danger of physical harm, though he could have been sentenced to imprisonment.

The Inquisition found a note from the 1616 Commission papers saying that Galileo had been formally warned not to hold, teach or discuss Copernicus. The words 'teach or discuss' were bad because, if the warning was official, then the *Dialogue* was clearly a violation. Where the 1616 note came from, is a mystery to this day. Galileo produced his letter from Bellarmine to disprove it.

Galileo's trial

The prosecution had a strong case. Galileo denied everything, but the book itself was proof enough. One of the judges persuaded Galileo to 'cop a plea', as we say nowadays. He admitted that he had argued too enthusiastically for Copernicus, inadvertently disobeyed the 1616 decision and, in mature reflection, now saw that he was wrong. Galileo claimed always to have held Ptolemy's system to be a fact, and used Copernicus only to 'save the appearances'. Everyone knew that this was a lie, but it got Galileo off the hook.

Now what do you think the Inquisition decided, and why?

'Eppur si muove' (But it moves)

The Inquisition's sentence was lenient and reasonable. It ignored the obvious fact that Galileo was lying about his real views, and demanded only that he solemnly deny the system of Copernicus, and be imprisoned for as long as the Inquisition decided.

On 22 June 1633, Galileo complied. Legend says that he muttered in Italian under his breath as he signed: *Eppur si muove* ('but it moves' – a reference to the movement of the earth). There is no evidence that he said anything. It is highly unlikely – given the circumstances – that he did. Finally, the Inquisition allowed him to return to his own home in Tuscany under house arrest. Urban VIII said he did not want to cause him unnecessary distress. Galileo remained a faithful Catholic for the rest of his life. He died in 1642.

HAPPY ENDING (SORT OF...)

Resources for further study
See teacher's text on CD-Rom for further suggestions.

Galileo spent his last decade going gradually blind, fretting in confinement, receiving visitors, and writing up his life's work. Barred from discussing the heavens, Galileo turned his attention to earth. He directly addressed the riddle: How to explain the movement of anything?

Aristotle had supplied a coherent explanation. Stability was natural; everything possessed a place of rest; motion needed a cause; a cause had to be in direct contact with the object in motion; heavenly motion was perfect and circular; natural earthly motion was downwards, if material, and upwards, if spiritual; heavy objects fall more quickly than light objects, and so on.

Assignment

Describe Galileo's second investigation (1632-3). Why do you think he complied in 1633?

Galileo had experimented to determine the laws of falling objects and the paths of projected ones. The story is that he once dropped two objects (a light one and a heavy one) from the top of the Tower of Pisa to show that they arrived at the ground at exactly the same time. Now in old age and confined to his quarters, he produced his outstanding scientific book: *Dialogue Concerning the Two New Sciences*.

The two sciences in question were the strength of materials and the laws of motion. In these books, the secrets of Galileo's genius are obvious: his application of mathematics to the physical world and his use of physical experiment. He demonstrated that all motion in the heavens and on earth, of comets and planets and moons, and of cannonballs and arrows and raindrops, is, in principle, the same. The final irony is that, nearly blind, Galileo demonstrated that he had seen further than anyone else.

Upshot

The Galileo Affair made the relationship between science and religion much more complicated. Galileo is frequently portrayed as a martyr for science, persecuted by the backward religious authorities of the Catholic Church. The reality was never so simple.

The personalities were cantankerous (Galileo more than anyone else involved). The principles of biblical interpretation were unclear, the science was uncertain, the theology was disputed, the politics was volatile, and academic rivalry was acute. All the ingredients were present for an explosion that no one wanted.

A fair verdict is that the Galileo Affair was a personal dispute set in a situation of professional rivalry mixed in with philosophical, religious and political reverberations that went far beyond the scientific and theological context that its participants assumed.

Neither Pope Paul V nor Urban VIII nor the Catholic Church ever pronounced the Copernican system as formally heretical, though many theological experts at the time thought that they should. Neither was Galileo blamed for discussing the

Copernican system, or for using it for calculating the movements of the planets. He was guilty of presenting it as fact and pushing its implications for biblical interpretation.

GALILEO'S PROBLEM

Galileo's problem was that he went outside his field. Academics and professors are always very jealous of their patch, and resent anyone who is not an expert saying anything about it. Making comments about the Bible was the business of a theologian, not one for a layman like Galileo, even if he was a scientist.

He had another problem. Galileo's observations did not in fact settle the Copernicus question. The calculations could be based on another model than the circular orbit of the earth around the sun, which Galileo espoused. In the end, that proved to be the case. Galileo's contemporary, Johannes Kepler, eventually demonstrated that the planetary orbits are not circles at all, but ellipses.

Johannes Kepler

Galileo's tomb

It is ironic that Galileo's most famous statement that the Bible does not tell us how the heavens go, but how to go to heaven, has proved correct as a matter of Bible interpretation. That he was only partly correct on the astronomy is the greatest irony of all.

The Vatican authorities had blundered with the Galileo Affair. There were indeed political, pastoral and religious reasons for confused thinking. But the Inquisition had taken a stand on a scientific question. The theologians had gone into the laboratory. This was a big mistake and it was to wrong-foot Catholic theology for centuries. The Catholic Church was depicted as backward, defensive, ignorant and unprogressive. This is the criticism that you will hear today, almost four hundred years later.

Pope John Paul II set up another Pontifical Commission to review the Galileo Affair and, so far as the Catholic Church was concerned, to draw the lesson from it. On Hallowe'en 1992, the Commission reported that the Inquisition had made an error to 'transpose a question of factual observation into the realm of faith'. Pope John Paul II himself apologised for the miscarriage of justice towards Galileo.

Assignments

1. Present a portrait of the world from which Galileo's ideas emerged.
2. Summarise Galileo's main findings and ideas.

Revision of Important Terms

Look up the following terms which you have come across in this chapter and briefly explain each one. Each of these terms is printed in bold in the text.

Thought experiment, Critical experiment, The Two Books, Literal interpretation of the Bible, Accommodated sense of the Bible, Inquisition.

Resources for further study
See teacher's text on CD-Rom for further suggestions.

In summary...

Galileo used accurate observation, precise measurement and clear reporting of discoveries to advance scientific knowledge. His astronomical sightings, with the newly invented telescope, excited great interest in science, and publicity for himself. It also drew opposition from Catholic teachers and preachers, who thought that his ideas challenged the Bible. Galileo was naïve to get involved directly in the controversy, and he suffered for it. The Catholic Church also was damaged by the controversy by appearing to oppose the emerging scientific enterprise.

Chapter 5

Scientific Revolution to Enlightenment (Science versus Religion)

'Tis all in pieces, all coherence gone.'

John Donne

Resources for further study
See teacher's text on CD-Rom for further suggestions.

> **In this chapter you will learn about...**
>
> ...two men of the seventeenth century: one French, the other English. The Frenchman René Descartes is called the 'Father of Modern Philosophy' because his approach to the question of knowledge defined the modern attitude to everything. The Englishman Isaac Newton was a true genius, laying down such foundations for mathematics, physics, astronomy and optics that he is sometimes thought of as the 'Father of Modern Science'. Between them, these two men changed the Medieval World-View through the Age of Enlightenment into the outlook that we are familiar with today.

This topic is also considered in **Section A, The Search for Meaning and Values**.

THE SCIENTIFIC REVOLUTION

A NEW PICTURE OF THE UNIVERSE

John Donne

In 1611, the year after Galileo's discoveries with his telescope, John Donne, the English poet, wrote *The Anatomy of the World*. Donne discerned the mood of the times and the way things were going. Confidence, especially in authority figures like princes and fathers, was gone. Donne said that: 'A new philosophy calls all in doubt.' He then penned this memorable line: 'Tis all in pieces, all coherence gone.'

'Coherence' means that something 'hangs together'. We say that ideas are 'coherent' if they are consistent. But the new view of the universe was 'all in pieces'. Things were splitting up. The Great Chain of Being was broken.

No one knew anything for certain. No authority could clear up the confusion. Every opinion could be challenged. You might be powerful or learned or old or wise or even successful, but the new ideas meant that the goals had changed, and there was a new game, on a level playing field. This 'new philosophy' was what historians call 'The Scientific Revolution'.

How do you think people felt about this scientific revolution back in the seventeenth century?

First of all, the people of the seventeenth century felt frightened. They had believed that the earth is the centre of the universe. Now they woke up to find that they were living on the third planet out from the sun, being whirled through an immense universe, with no idea about what else they were going to find out. So the new discoveries led to a certain fear.

Then, they felt confused. The old certainties were gone. A man believed that the sun went around the earth. His grandson knew that the earth went around the sun. He also knew that his grandfather was wrong. Nobody had all the answers. This led to a certain confusion.

RENÉ DESCARTES (1596-1650)

René Descartes was born in France at the end of the sixteenth century. As an eight-year-old boy, he went to a Jesuit school. He was a delicate and sickly child, who used to lie on till ten o'clock in the mornings, even at boarding school, thinking about philosophical problems. As he grew up into adulthood, he began to try to solve them.

René Descartes

When Descartes was only twenty-three years old, on the night of 10 November 1619, he had three dreams which convinced him that all knowledge is mathematical. The philosophical project on which he embarked for the rest of his life as a result of that vision earned him the title by which he is most often known: 'Father of Modern Philosophy'.

What struck the young man was the contrast between philosophy and mathematics. How could mathematics be so clear and certain, and philosophy be so woolly and vague? Descartes thought that philosophy could be made more distinct and simple.

This he set himself to do.

THE BOTTOM LINE IN KNOWLEDGE

Descartes' project was an ambitious one. He wanted to clear away all uncertainty and doubt. If there were any unreliable or questionable ideas in his head, then they had to go. It was as if a city decided to knock down and demolish all buildings that were not completely solid structures, that is, any that were not totally safe. Only a few houses could survive such a cull. And so it was with Descartes' ideas.

COGITO ERGO SUM... I THINK, THEREFORE I AM

René Descartes seems to be really stuck. How can he get out of this swamp of doubt? Where can he find a solid foothold of

Assignment

Research 'The Scientific Revolution' and its impact on the people at the time.

Group work

Descartes began with the only certainties he could find. Anything that could be wrong had to go. Let us try another thought experiment. What is the most certain thing you know? Let us pretend that we are René Descartes all those years ago.

Suppose you said that you know that you are alive! But that could be wrong. You could be dreaming, only imagining that you are alive. Often you dream that you are in places and doing things that are totally imaginary. How are you certain that you are not in a dream right now? A slim chance, all right, but that is still a chance. So it has to go.

Suppose you said that you are sure that you have a body and that you have senses with which you can see, hear, touch, taste and smell things! Surely they are certain knowledge? No. It sometimes happens that we see things that are not there, we hear sounds that do not exist, and so on. Our senses can fool us. Therefore, they may be wrong. So they have to go too.

For discussion

This had an enormous impact on modern scientific thinking. Can you work out what it is? (Here is a hint: Is the thing which doubts the same thing as René Descartes?)

certainty? Everything, it seems, can be doubted. Anything can be wrong.

Descartes then said something like this: 'Well, if I am wrong about my own life and about my sense knowledge, I still know one thing beyond all doubt! I am certain that I am doubtful. I am trying to work out this problem. I am thinking. This means that I must exist. And that is the most certain thing of all.' Descartes' argument was put into three famous words in Latin: **Cogito ergo sum** – translated as 'I think (Cogito) therefore (ergo) I am (sum)'.

BODY AND SOUL

René Descartes was a being made up of body and soul. He was a small man, with black hair, a weak chest, a big head and an impatient disposition. He was French, a brilliant mathematician, an original psychologist, a deep philosopher and a devout Catholic. He did a lot of things other than doubting and thinking, such as walking, sleeping, praying, talking, getting sick, lying in bed and so on. So René Descartes was a complex being with two aspects, bodily and spiritual.

But the *Cogito* proof for his existence only accepted as certain the fact that he *thought*, that he was a *thinking being*. His certain knowledge related only to the spiritual or mental or thinking side of his existence. The part of René Descartes that related to his body was still doubtful after the argument was over.

The unity that is René Descartes, or any human being, became 'The Ghost in the Machine'.

TWO KINDS OF BEING

This may not seem very important, but it divided the mental from the material in scientific thought. The world, after René Descartes, would be seen to contain two different kinds of being.

The first kind of being is the world of externals: that is, the length and breadth and depth and colour and sound and size and weight and momentum and velocity and force and all the bulk and mass and action and motion that fills the material universe.

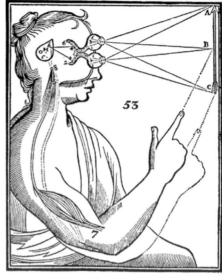

The second kind of being is the internal world, of thought, emotion, consciousness, imagination, ideas, reason, and all that we connect with the spiritual. This is the world of the thinking person, the *ego*, the 'I' of the 'I think, therefore I am'.

Dualism means that reality is composed of two fundamentally distinct kinds of being, so different that they are impossible to combine. Descartes had divided mind from matter, the subject (oneself, the *ego*, the 'I') from the object (the physical world), so sharply that it would be difficult in future to imagine how they could come together at all. This belief is referred to as **Cartesian dualism** ('Cartesian' is the adjective from Descartes, from the Latin version of his name.)

Cartesian dualism

PRIMARY AND SECONDARY QUALITIES

Descartes' method, however, had an even deeper and more lasting effect on scientific thinking and on European culture. He divided the soul from the body in the human person. He made a similar separation in the material world.

Descartes declared that everything we can observe has two kinds of quality: primary qualities and secondary qualities. **Primary qualities** are size, shape, dimension, speed, and things that we can measure mathematically. **Secondary qualities** are the subjective things, such as colour, sound, taste and touch.

The result has been that, up to the present day, people still regard physically measurable qualities as *more real* than other qualities that we might know and identify.

METHOD OF DOUBT

Descartes' approach is called the **'Method of Doubt'**. That means that he could only rely on the absolutely certain part of his knowledge. He must ignore a lot of what he knows, even though it is quite likely to be true too.

Descartes is ripping down all the rickety buildings in a city in order to replace them with strongly built structures. But he has torn down perfectly good buildings too, and he is left with very few houses, with no chance to build any more. He does this because he wants to argue against scepticism.

1. What happened to Descartes when he was twenty-three years old?
2. How did Descartes arrive at 'Cogito ergo sum'?
3. What was Descartes' notion of body and soul?
4. Explain 'Cartesian dualism'.
5. What do you understand by Descartes' 'Method of Doubt'?
6. What is scepticism?

For discussion

1. Would it be true to say that Descartes' ideas have shaped your thinking? Do you think of material things as 'more real' and spiritual things as 'less real'? Explain your answer.
2. Outline Descartes' theory and explain its importance for science and religion.

Resources for further study
See teacher's text on CD-Rom for further suggestions.

Isaac Newton

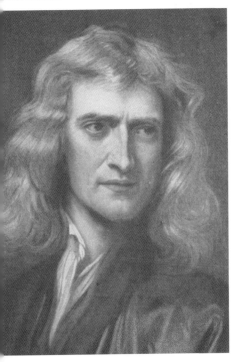

SCEPTICISM

Scepticism is an attitude of universal doubt whereby evidence and conclusive proof is required for every single judgement. Sceptical thinking was very common in the seventeenth century, as people lost faith in all authority, religious, political, intellectual and philosophical.

Descartes himself, as he was a devout Christian and a keen scientist, wanted to hold the truths of both religion and reason. His method, however, had the effect of making the individual the only judge as to the truth of anything. He accepted no evidence that could not be personally and completely checked out from the start. So by adopting the 'Method of Doubt', Descartes opened the door to a more thoroughgoing scepticism and, eventually, to complete atheism.

DEATH OF DESCARTES

Descartes' fame travelled far and wide. Queen Christina of Sweden hired him to travel to Stockholm and teach her philosophy. Because she was a busy woman, she arranged that classes should start at five in the morning. Descartes was living in the French Embassy and he had to go out into the cold to keep his appointment. Returning in the early morning chill in early 1650, poor René Descartes caught a lung infection, and he died a few days later of pneumonia, on 11 February. He was fifty-four years old.

ISAAC NEWTON (1642-1727)

(The material on Isaac Newton, from here to end p. 69, is for Higher Level students only.)

In 1642, the year that Galileo died in Florence in Italy, Isaac Newton was born in Lincolnshire in England. As a young pupil, he was described as 'idle' and 'inattentive'. But his school work eventually improved sufficiently for him to be sent to Cambridge University. While he was taking careful notes in the middle of a university lecture on Aristotle in 1663 (at the age of twenty-one), he quit the note-taking, skipped ahead to a new page, put a title 'Some Questions in Philosophy' at the top, followed it with a motto 'I am a friend to Plato and Aristotle but more a friend to truth', and began to write his own independently researched investigations. By the time he earned his degree, he had written a number of studies in philosophy and science.

Newton's most inventive year came in 1665 and 1666 when he was only twenty-three years old. (You remember that René Descartes had his wonderful dream when he was twenty-three?) A plague sent Newton home from Cambridge, and it was there that he enjoyed his *annus mirabilis* (miraculous year). Newton tells us that when he saw an apple fall to the ground in his orchard, the insight came to him that both the moon in the sky and objects falling to the ground might be drawn by the same force of **gravity**. His conclusion (that the same scientific theory applies both in the heavens and on the earth) was the basis for his life's work and for his lasting significance.

THE THREE LAWS OF MOTION

This was the age of artillery. Armies were developing bigger and bigger cannon, and soldiers were keen to find out how to aim their guns more accurately. Galileo had already worked on projectiles and noted that their path was always a parabola. (A parabola is the cross-section of a cone.)

Newton conducted a famous thought experiment (just like Galileo). He imagined a large cannon firing a cannonball from the top of a very high mountain. It could happen that at a sufficient speed, the roundness of the earth would ensure that

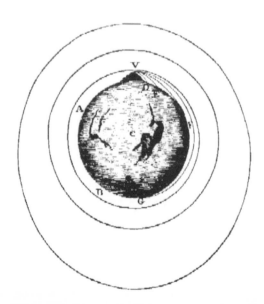

Newton's cannon thought experiment

the cannonball would never strike the ground at all. In other words, the cannonball could become a small artificial moon circling the earth for ever. Newton's thought experiment remained imaginary until 1958, when the USSR launched *Sputnik*, the first artificial satellite, into earth orbit. And the calculations of speed, angle of flight and so on, followed exactly from Newton's theory.

Arising from his calculations, Newton proposed his famous three laws of motion, which everybody learns in Physics class today. The really important insight that Newton brought to the study of the earth, planets and stars is that *everything that moves obeys the three universal laws of motion.*

ACTION AT A DISTANCE

Isaac Newton had crossed an important line in science. The medieval scientists could only imagine things moving if they were pushed. You had to exert direct pressure on an object to move it. You could not have '**action at a distance**'.

Newton, however, had conceived of objects as 'remaining in uniform motion in a straight line', and he had introduced the concept of 'force', such as gravity, which could draw or pull an object from a distance. Gravity is an example of 'action at a distance'.

The force that made the apple fall to the ground in Newton's garden is the same force that keeps the moon in its place circling the earth, and the earth in its place circling the sun, and the comets whirling in from outer reaches of the universe. All of the heavenly objects move in regular paths, and mathematics can calculate their speed, estimate their forces of attraction to one another, and accurately predict their future movements.

In the same way, movements of objects here on earth can be calculated and predicted. Newton had achieved a grand unifying system, based on mathematics. On this foundation, a new vision of the universe would be built: the Newtonian world-view.

For discussion

1. What do you think space is?
2. How do you imagine the space that contains everything? Is it a place? Does it contain everything? Is it like a big box?
3. What happens when you come to the edge of everything that exists? Is there no more space?

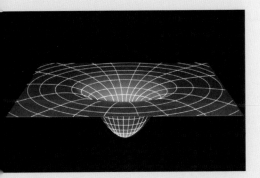

SPACE

Newton started from 'clear and distinct ideas', but sometimes he had to make up his new ones. Some new ideas, though, had old names, like space and time. These ideas are very important for the relationship between science and religion.

You probably think of space as 'containing' everything in some way. Maybe you don't think of it like a box, with sides and edges, and perhaps you imagine it as just coming to an end, with nothing beyond, like the edge of the land when one arrives at the coast. Or you may think of it in terms of a big sphere, that just comes to an end, and outside you can see nothing.

Maybe you think of space as independent of any particular thing. In other words, space starts a great distance away in one direction, goes past where we are now, and stretches out for zillions of miles in the other direction; everything that we call 'material reality' is floating and flying around in between. Thus it would be quite easy to imagine space as 'holding', 'containing' or at least 'surrounding' everything.

This is Newton's idea of space, as he described it. Newton made **space** into a framework or container for everything, extending beyond everything, but unrelated to anything. Space would exist even if nothing ever was in it.

This was quite different from the ancient idea of space. For the ancient and medieval thinkers, space existed only when things existed. Without things, there would be no space between them, so to speak, and no space around them. Space was not a pre-existing container, but the distance between and the area around whatever things happened to exist.

Time

The other distinct Newtonian idea concerned time. Let us now take some time to think about time...

You probably think of time as unending. The passing of time is an unchanging rhythm, 'tick-tock, tick-tock', like the 'Grandfather's Clock'. You may think of time as having no beginning, stretching back for unimaginable ages, and set to keep on going on for ever and ever and ever. Like a great river in flow, time courses on in a steady stream, carrying all in its surge, bearing everything and everyone from the past through the fleeting present into the mysteries of the yet-to-come.

This was Newton's idea of **time**: independent of things existing or of events happening in it, time extends uniformly and infinitely, with no beginning and no end, progressing at a steady pace, and everything that happens, if it happens, occurs within it.

Once again, Newton's 'clear and distinct idea' was described quite differently from the 'time' as

For discussion

1. What do you think time is?
2. How do you imagine time? Is it a river? Does it just keep rolling along?
3. What happens when you come to the end of time? Is there no more time?
5. How do you think time relates to eternity?

68

Questions

1. What happened to Newton at the age of twenty-three?
2. What was his famous thought experiment with the cannonball?
3. What was Newton's idea of space?
4. What was Newton's idea of time?

For discussion

Newton's world-view is the one that most people hold today, it seems. Check this out in discussion with your friends, and with your parents/ guardians and neighbours.

Strasburg Clock

Assignment

Write an essay on the 'Newtonian world-view', explaining its importance for the relationship between science and religion.

discussed by the ancient and medieval philosophers before him.

Aristotle had said that we recognise the passage of time only when we notice change. Something has to change for time to happen: either the clock hands move, or the sun sets, or we grow older or bigger. Did you ever notice that a school class can (sometimes) drag on and on until it seems never to end? Forty or forty-five minutes can feel like eternity! And at other times, time flies. A party, an absorbing TV programme or film, a holiday, all are over in a flash. We do not feel time as flowing uniformly at all. Time speeds up, or slows down, depending on the things that are changing, or not changing, around us. This is the way the ancient and medieval thinkers regarded time. Time was the measure of change.

NEWTON'S WORLD-VIEW

Newton transformed how humans saw the universe. If space is the box, time is the beat. The framework of space is huge. The pace of time is unyielding, relentless and inevitable. Both are inhuman, heartless and cold. In a word, they are mechanical.

The **Newtonian world-view** takes the place of the medieval world-view. The world is a great machine, a mechanical engine, following regular laws, organised by simple principles, predictable, enormous and ancient, with an unimaginable future.

For the scientist, the universe is a well-ordered, stable set of parts, well-oiled cogs and wheels, and, in theory, science could predict the future motion of any particle or being once its position, velocity and mass has been accurately measured. No longer is there mystery or magic or awe or terror in the face of divinity or demon or spirit. There is nothing out there except hunks of rock and the motion of matter through space and time.

In this world-view, humans are no longer at the centre of the universe. They are tiny spectators of an immense and overwhelming system. It may be possible that they can understand it, but not relate to it; that they can conquer it, but not love it; that they can wonder at it, but not adore its creator.

(End of Higher Level material)

69

THE ENLIGHTENMENT

DISAPPEARANCE OF GOD

René Descartes was a good Catholic. He wanted to avoid the trouble with theologians that Galileo had experienced, so he did not publish his own writing on the nature of the universe. Descartes was being prudent. He was also expressing his own deep religious sense.

For Descartes, God was at the centre of things. Descartes believed that the idea of God is one of the few clear and distinct ideas the human mind can rely on. God cannot deceive us. But once you have thought of the idea of God, you do not need God thereafter; you can keep going with philosophy and science. The door was open for God to leave, for the **'disappearance of God'**.

Isaac Newton was also a very religious man, though he did not attend church much. He was an Anglican by birth, but he thought deeply about religious things as well as about science. He kept an important role for God in his picture of the universe. Newton was certain that God is needed as a cause for the universe. Such a complicated design could not be explained by natural causes alone.

God enacted the laws by which the universe works. But is God needed so that it continues to work? Newton thought that God is always necessary. God is needed to keep the planets and stars organised; otherwise they would clump together or scatter throughout space. Newton had sufficient appreciation of the messiness of things to know that the universe could not be as precise as a giant clock, and he thought that God would have to repair the mechanism.

But then God could become redundant. The idea of the clock was too persuasive. The Divine Clock-Maker was not needed for maintenance. Once God made the universe, it would continue for ever without repair. God could, finally, disappear from view.

THE ENLIGHTENMENT

The eighteenth century is called **'The Age of Enlightenment'**. What did that mean? The scientists and thinkers of the Scientific Revolution considered themselves more enlightened than their contemporaries and their predecessors. They thought that they knew more than those before them or around them. They were confident that the mind could discover new truths about the world.

This topic is also considered in **Section A, The Search for Meaning and Values** and **Section I, Religion: The Irish Experience**.

Assignment

An Irishman named Robert Boyle, known as the 'Father of Modern Chemistry and Son of the Earl of Cork', was a very important figure in the Enlightenment and the scientific life of England. He also had very definite views about religion. Find out what Robert Boyle thought about science and religion.

Robert Boyle

They were no longer relying on the past or on authority or on religion for answers. People made up their minds for themselves and decided the conduct of their own lives, individually and socially. They were sure that they knew how to do that, even if others were still locked in ignorance, superstition and oppression. Finally, the Enlightenment thinkers were happy that their ideas, if practised, would lead to a better society.

RATIONAL RELIGION

Confidence and enthusiasm for human ability and the power of reason during the Enlightenment extended to religion. Eighteenth-century thinkers were optimistic that rational methods and a scientific approach would help them to achieve a newer, wiser and more just sense of God. Previous centuries had been full of sectarian strife and vicious religious wars. This bitter conflict convinced Europeans that religion can cause violence, and that the world needs reasonable human beings to remove fanaticism and bring peace.

'**Rational religion**', that is, religion without the Bible, traditional authority or revelation, avoids dogmatism, authoritarianism and superstition. Anyone can have it, of any faith or of none. Everyone can agree to it. Rational religion means that belief in God and morality can be established separately from faith. Catholics and Protestants, Jews and Muslims, religious people and atheists could find common ground in reason. Rational religion provides 'the clear and distinct ideas' on which revealed, scriptural and historical religions build. Or so the philosophers of the Enlightenment hoped.

THE TWO BOOKS AGAIN

The Two Books argument claimed that God had written revealed truth in the Book of the Word – the Bible or Sacred Scripture— and that God had also produced the Book of the World – the universe, the natural and created world. During the seventeenth and eighteenth centuries, the Two Books argument went through three stages.

Cardinal Bellarmine

In the first stage, theologians and scientists assumed that both Books should be treated equally. There is only one truth, and things written in the Bible and in the universe ought to agree. If there were a contradiction, then the Bible should be believed firmly, until the scientific truth was proved beyond doubt. This was how Cardinal Bellarmine and his friends were advising Galileo.

The second stage puts the Book of the World before the Book of the Word. Reason uncovers the deepest truths: the existence

Assignments

1. Explain what you understand by the 'Age of Enlightenment'?
2. Write a note on 'rational religion'.
3. How do you account for the disappearance of God during the 'Age of Enlightenment'?

of a Creator, the immortality of the soul, and the nature of moral obligation. Reason is the basic way of finding out about God and the universe. What we know by our reason is clearer than the truths of the Bible.

The third stage follows. The Bible is unnecessary. Not only is scientific knowledge derived from the world easier to understand than the Bible, it is more certain. What we read in the Bible is faith, and that is less certain. It may only be our opinion.

The eighteenth-century French mathematician Pierre Laplace presented Napoleon with his treatise on the movements of the celestial bodies. Napoleon remarked that in all the pages there was no reference to the Creator of the universe. Laplace allegedly replied: 'Sire, I have no need for that hypothesis.'

Pierre Laplace

NATURAL THEOLOGY

This topic is also considered in **Section C, World Religions**.

William Paley, an Anglican theologian and bishop, told this story: 'Suppose that on a country walk we find a watch. We look at it. We note that its purpose is to tell the time of the day. We conclude that this machine had a maker. Someone manufactured it. It was designed.'

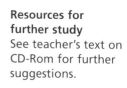

Resources for further study
See teacher's text on CD-Rom for further suggestions.

When we look around us at the world, is it not the same? It too is clearly the result of design. **Design** is the intelligent and systematic arrangement of parts in

William Paley

a purposeful whole. Design leads us to the existence of a mind to think up the design, a person to appreciate its purpose, and an agent to bring it into existence.

This is an example of natural theology, because it relies entirely upon nature. **Natural theology** is the attempt to attain knowledge of God without revelation, or authority, or tradition.

Question

What is the difference between the watchmaker making the watch, and God creating the universe? In other words, does God make the world in the same way as a watchmaker makes a watch?

But there is a big problem with natural theology. Can you see it? Perhaps it would be good to pause here and discuss, or at least think about, one probing question. (See 'Question' on left.)

DEISM, THEISM AND ATHEISM

The watch is separate from the watchmaker once the watch-making is finished. The watchmaker is no longer needed to keep the watch in existence. The watchmaker is needed only at the beginning, when the watch is being made. This is the difference between the work of the Creator and that of a watchmaker. God is needed even after the world has been started up.

The belief that God is the maker only at the start of the world is called **deism**. ('Deism' comes from the Latin word for God.) **Deism** was a very popular view throughout the eighteenth-century Enlightenment.

For deists, God is not active in the universe now. If God is no longer active, it is a short step to say that God is not present at all. A God who is not here might as well not exist. Showing that God exists through the evidence of the natural world, like William Paley did, ends up showing that God may exist, but that it does not matter anyway.

Theism is the belief that God is the creator of the world; that is, that God made it from nothing and sustains it in being at all times. ('Theism' comes from the *Greek* word for God.)

Atheism ('A' is the prefix that means 'not' in Greek) is the belief that there is no God at all.

If we do not recognise our continuing dependence on God, theism can be reduced to deism. Then deism easily changes to atheism.

Assignments

1. Compose a survey or interview questions that you can give to groups in your school or neighbourhood to find out which is the most common belief among young people of your acquaintance: theism, deism or atheism?

2. Describe one major development in science and one major development in religion at the time of the Enlightenment.

Revision of Important Terms

Look up the following terms which you have come across in this chapter and briefly explain each one. Each of these terms is printed in bold in the text.

Cogito ergo sum, Dualism, Cartesian dualism, Primary qualities, Secondary qualities, Method of Doubt, Scepticism, Gravity, Action at a distance, Space, Time, Newtonian world-view, Disappearance of God, Age of Enlightenment, Rational religion, Design, Natural theology, Deism, Theism, Atheism.

In summary...

In this chapter, we learned about the crucial contributions of Descartes and Newton to the Enlightenment and, therefore, to the encounter between science and religion. Descartes introduced the 'Method of Doubt' by which he hoped to counter scepticism. His *Cogito* argument attempted to establish a certain foundation for all knowledge, but it resulted in dividing reality into the spiritual and the material. The spiritual was the realm of opinion and faith; the material was the measurable, scientific and more certain. Newton developed this approach into a consistent philosophical, mathematical and scientific system, which provided the world-view for the next three centuries. Finally, we noted that natural theology or rational religion neither convinced sceptics nor halted the 'disappearance of God' from European thought.

Chapter 6

Darwin and Evolution (Science and Religion in Tension)

'Man with all his noble qualities, ...with his god-like intellect which has penetrated into the movements and constitution of the solar system – with all these exalted powers – still bears in his bodily frame the indelible stamp of his lowly origin.'

Charles Darwin, *The Descent of Man*

Resources for further study
See teacher's text on CD-Rom for
further suggestions.

This topic is also considered in
**Section A, The Search for Meaning
and Values** and **Section C, World
Religions**.

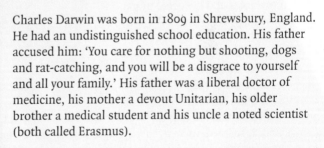

In this chapter you will learn about...

*...how to enter into the nineteenth-century discussions concerning
evolution. The story of Charles Darwin is a fascinating one, from
young student to elder statesman of science, as he travels the world
on the Beagle and embarks on a journey of scientific discovery. This
will lead to a serious challenge to scientific and religious thought on
many levels. We trace the reaction to Darwin's ideas into the present
century.*

CHARLES DARWIN (1809-1882)

Charles Darwin was born in 1809 in Shrewsbury, England.
He had an undistinguished school education. His father
accused him: 'You care for nothing but shooting, dogs
and rat-catching, and you will be a disgrace to yourself
and all your family.' His father was a liberal doctor of
medicine, his mother a devout Unitarian, his older
brother a medical student and his uncle a noted scientist
(both called Erasmus).

Charles certainly did not know what to do with his life;
his father was right about that. After a few false starts,
first in medicine (he was queasy around dissections) and
then in theology (he was not very religious), Darwin
found his feet in the new and growing sciences of zoology
and geology. He particularly enjoyed field trips with his
professors, searching for interesting specimens,
cataloguing his discoveries and trying to understand his
results.

The problem was that there was, at that time, no clear career which would earn a respectable living for a naturalist like Darwin. Then in August 1831, at the age of twenty-two (almost twenty-three), came the decisive moment of Charles Darwin's young life. He received an invitation to go on a round-the-world expedition, as the scientific companion to Captain Fitzroy of the Royal Navy ship, the *Beagle*. Darwin accepted and, for the next five years, he circled the globe, collecting rocks and samples of animal life, drawing diagrams and writing scientific notes. At each port of call, he shipped home to England a load of material. The young naturalist eventually returned home to sort out his collection, report his more interesting findings and try to make sense of it all. He was to spend the rest of his life doing just that.

The Beagle

FASCINATING OBSERVATIONS

Probably the most interesting of his findings concerned the birds and animals of a small group of islands in the Pacific Ocean off the coast of South America. The Galapagos Islands would enter history, forever connected with Charles Darwin and the *Beagle*. They were hardly more than outcrops of rock in the ocean, but they provided a harsh and barren home for many strange forms of bird, turtle and plant. Darwin became aware that fascinating things were going on there. It was, however, only when he returned to England that he realised quite how fascinating they were. As often happens with scientists, and other researchers, he realised too late that he should have taken more notes and collected more samples while he was there.

Galapagos Islands

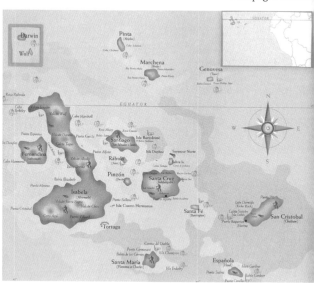

In particular, the young Darwin learned a lot about the Galapagos Island finches. Bird experts helped him to identify the different varieties of finch, and he suddenly noticed that each variety was confined to its own island. It seemed, indeed, that a single kind of finch had found its way to the archipelago, but that it then developed into separate varieties according to the different conditions on the isolated islands. This was an astonishing clue to have come upon.

CHANGING IDEAS

If you guessed that it was surprising to Darwin because the changing finches were an illustration of evolution in action, you are half right!

Question

Why do you think Darwin's observation regarding finches was so astonishing for him? Take a moment to think of reasons why he was surprised.

Jean-Pierre Lamarck

Darwin already knew about evolution. His uncle Erasmus had, in fact, proposed an evolutionary theory fifty years before. But there was an essential difference between that idea of evolution and what he was to make of it.

The idea of evolution in the early nineteenth century stemmed from the work of a French naturalist named Jean-Pierre Lamarck (1744-1829). Lamarck believed that learned characteristics could be passed on to offspring. In other words, if you were not very mathematically talented, but needed to be, and by hard work and diligence managed to get your Leaving Certificate in Honours Maths, then it was possible that your children would be more talented at mathematics than you were. You would have passed on to them the skill that you learned. It sounded very plausible.

Lamarck's idea of evolution included the notion of *purpose.* (You must, after all, *want* to get good at mathematics.) Nineteenth-century thinkers were very convinced of progress. For them, the whole of life had a goal and, therefore, evolution too must have a purpose and direction. **Lamarckism** – the inheritance of acquired characteristics – fitted into that world-view very well.

Archbishop James Ussher

Charles Lyell

THE 'AGE OF THE EARTH' QUESTION

If you know exactly where you are going, you can get there quicker. That is true of travel; it is also true of human development. If evolution were purposeful, it could be accomplished in a relatively short space of time, say, under ten thousand years.

Nineteenth-century thinkers thought that the span of recorded history was less than that. The events narrated in the Bible, for instance, occurred only within the last six thousand years, and creation happens in the first chapter of the first book of Genesis. As good Bible Christians, they wanted the Bible to agree with the latest scientific knowledge.

Archbishop James Ussher (1581-1656), of Armagh and Trinity College, Dublin, had carefully calculated the time-line for biblical history, and concluded that the creation of the world happened on Sunday, 23 October 4004 BCE. Ussher's dating is often laughed at now, but in its time, this was a genuinely scientific effort. The method is called **concordism**, the attempted accommodation of scientific knowledge with the corresponding information from the Sacred Scriptures.

But there were natural clues that the world was much older than that. Charles Lyell (1797-1875) wrote an influential book on geology in 1830. He showed that the earth was much older. Lyell's book excited little controversy but much interest ·

because it was about rocks and stones, even though it raised questions about the development of animals. It was a major influence on the young Darwin as he set out on the *Beagle*.

Naturalists had to explain the puzzle of how the world's animals developed. At the time of Darwin, they held two views: **catastrophism** – that the world's flora and fauna resulted from disasters, such as the universal flood in the Bible; and **uniformism** – that the world was formed in the past by processes still operating now. Charles Lyell, for example, argued for uniformism.

A NEW EXPLANATION

Charles Darwin was beginning to glimpse the possibility of another mechanism that would cause new kinds of being to emerge, and the new mechanism had no place for purpose. He had read Thomas Malthus' famous book *Essay on the Principle of Population*. Malthus argued that competition for scarce resources reduced populations and ensured that only the fittest would survive, because the weak were, so to speak, weeded out.

SURVIVAL OF THE FITTEST

Darwin's geology studies and personal observations had shown him **fossils** (animal forms preserved in ancient rocks) of long-extinct species. How had those species (like dinosaurs, for instance) failed to survive?

Thomas Malthus

Questions

1. What decisive moment came in Darwin's life at age twenty-two?
2. Describe his adventures and observations on the *Beagle* over the next five years.
3. Briefly explain Lamarckism.
4. Distinguish between 'catastrophism' and 'uniformism'.

Fossils

Assignment

Write a note on Darwin's notion of the 'survival of the fittest'.

Darwin surmised that those species became extinct because they were less adapted to their environment than their competitors. If the environment changed, then an advantage in a previous situation could become a disadvantage in the new situation. The animal then became less likely to survive in the competition for resources.

On the other hand, a change in the animal's body that put it at an advantage in the struggle for survival, would be more likely to be passed on to its offspring. The change would be the beginning of a new branch of descendants. This process is called the **'survival of the fittest'**.

EVOLUTION

Darwin's **theory of evolution** states that random variations, with successful adaptations, in isolated environments, under conditions of scarce resources, leads to the development of new species.

The difference with Lamarckian evolution is that purpose plays no part in the process.

What astonished Charles Darwin about the finches and other specimens on the Galapagos Islands was that they might be evidence of that explanation in action. Darwin thought that they could provide examples of new species beginning.

ORIGIN OF SPECIES, 1859

Darwin mulled over his ideas for many years. He shared them with selected members of his family and close friends, but he did not publish them officially. He seemed reluctant to go public, and this might have been because religious and intellectual leaders were engaged in controversy at that time. Darwin did not want to be involved in any disputes and so he steered very clear of them.

small ground finch medium ground finch large ground finch

sharp-beaked ground finch cactus finch large cactus finch

small tree finch large tree finch? vegetarian finch

woodpecker finch warbler finch

Different types of finch

In 1858, however, another naturalist, Alfred Wallace, told him that he intended to publish a theory on evolution similar to Darwin's. The two arranged that they would submit joint papers to the Royal Society on 1 July that year. The two papers caused no controversy at all. So, Darwin proceeded to publish his full-length book *Origin of Species*, which came out in 1859. He sent a copy to Wallace with the ironic comment: 'God knows what the public will think.'

Alfred Wallace

NATURAL SELECTION

For centuries, people had been well aware of the practice of breeding. By dint of careful selection, breeders and gardeners had developed varieties of animals and plants with special characteristics. This was called **'artificial selection'**.

Darwin borrowed the name for his own theory, which he called **'natural selection'**. He claimed that natural selection accounted for more than the refinement of qualities of already defined species. Natural selection, according to Darwin, could be a sufficient explanation for the appearance of entirely new species.

Resources for further study
See teacher's text on CD-Rom for further suggestions.

Natural selection works like this. Overpopulation means that there are more individuals than can be supported by resources, which leads directly to a struggle for existence, as individuals compete for the same resources. The result is natural balance. Changes in conditions, however, inevitably occur at some time or other. For example, the climate grows colder, or hotter, or a fresh rival appears, or an earthquake strikes. This leads to new conflict over resources. Animals that possess random advantages, because of individual variations, are more likely to survive, and more likely to pass on their advantageous variations to descendants. Over time, these individual advantageous variations emerge in new species.

Evolution of the horse

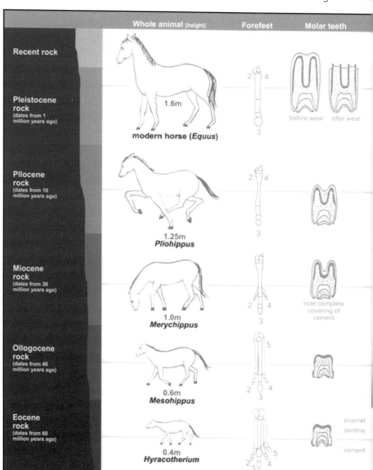

IMPLICATIONS

There are three points to be noted about natural selection.

The first point is that natural selection appears to eliminate all consideration of design. The result *looks* designed, but apparently is not. It seems to eliminate any necessity for purpose, and, of course, for the Will of God.

The second point is that natural selection is still in action today. Darwin's theory of evolution sided with the uniformitarians.

The third point is that there is no progress built into the process. Evolution can go in either direction. It is a matter of random variation and environmental adaptation. The process could go either way.

REACTION TO 'ORIGIN OF SPECIES'

Darwin's book did excite comment and discussion when it came out. It was reviewed passionately and energetically, favourably and unfavourably. Readers were impressed by the persuasive writing, by the multitude of examples and illustrations, and by the overarching theory.

Darwin's argument was that natural selection explained things better than any other theory; much better, in particular, than special creation. **Special creation** proposed, following the book of Genesis, that God created each species separately, and that, since then, species did not change, but were 'immutable'. Special creation did not explain fossils of long-extinct species.

Darwin did not deny God in the *Origin of Species*. He skirted around the topic carefully. He professed to find 'grandeur' in the vision of creatures evolving from one or a few forms. He used the words 'God' and 'Creator' in his book, and quoted an anonymous theologian that there was no contradiction between evolution and creation.

Critics immediately spotted the exclusion of purpose. Others noticed that he had installed chance, or variation, or nature, as the explanation, in place of God. Some scientists said that he had proved only the plausibility of his theory ('it could be so') rather than its necessity ('it must be so').

Darwin's support, however, was keen and enthusiastic. It was not true that all scientists were for him, and all theologians against him, but those scientists who were for him, were very committed. Science was fighting for recognition in the universities, and some scientists saw a chance to 'do down' the

Assignments

1. Explain Darwin's theory of evolution.
2. What do you understand by 'artificial selection' and 'natural selection'?
3. Discuss 'natural selection' in relation to 'special creation'.

established educational powers, if they could advance the cause of evolution.

THE OXFORD DEBATE

The British Association for the Advancement of Science organised its Annual General Meeting in 1860 in the Natural History Museum of Oxford University on the subject of evolution. The building that houses the Museum had been built in 1860, and the AGM marked its opening. A famous debate was staged before 700 people. The room displays a commemorative plaque: 'A meeting of the British Association held 30 June 1860 within this door was the scene of the memorable debate on evolution between Samuel Wilberforce Bishop of Oxford and Thomas Henry Huxley.'

The Oxford University Museum of Natural History, renowned for its spectacular neo-Gothic architecture

Neither Charles Darwin nor Alfred Wallace was present.

There are at least two versions of what happened. The first is Thomas Huxley's account thirty years afterwards. Bishop Wilberforce attacked the theory of evolution with scorn, with the support of the audience. During the talk, he asked Huxley if it was his grandfather or grand*mother* who had descended from an ape. Huxley then stood up and replied with a scientific argument, commenting that given the choice, he would prefer to have the ape as grandfather, than to be the descendant of an intelligent man who would introduce ridicule into a serious scientific discussion. This won many of the crowd over, and the bishop was defeated. Rational science had overcome backward religion.

Thomas Huxley

But historians are not clear if that really happened. There are contemporary reports in magazines, and some from other spectators. None confirms Huxley's version exactly. Wilberforce's speech was probably scientific criticism, and he, indeed, may have indulged in a personal insult. But the debate was not as noteworthy at the time as it became in memory. Huxley was barely audible to the audience, and public address systems, of course, were unknown. In all likelihood, the debate was a draw.

Plaque outside the room where the Huxley–Wilberforce encounter took place

Questions

1. Why do you think the Oxford Debate became such a myth?
2. Would such a debate have any relevance today? Explain your answer.

Evolution of man

Right: Westminster Cathedral, which houses Darwin's tomb (below)

The debate was made into a symbol of the conquest of reason over superstition, and claimed as a victory in the warfare between science and religion. Everyone came to assume that humankind had evolved, even if they were not quite sure how it happened, and many were certain that religion had been discredited at the Oxford Debate.

DESCENT OF MAN, 1871

The *Origin of Species* had not dealt with the evolution of human beings. Darwin filled the gap in 1871 with his book *Descent of Man*. Nevertheless, by the time the book was published, public opinion was prepared for the idea of human evolution.

Personally, Darwin had gradually lost his own religious faith, and he admitted, late in life, to being **agnostic** (a term coined by Huxley, meaning one who *does not know* if there is a God or not). But Darwin himself was never scandalously controversial. He always craved the quiet life, and he died peacefully at home from a heart attack on 19 April 1882. He was accorded a full public funeral, at Westminster Abbey, and he is buried there among the great and the good of England.

AFTER EVOLUTION

CHALLENGE TO RELIGION

Darwin's theory of evolution was seen at the time, as challenging religion. Some challenges could be countered by reformulating theological ideas, or by adapting scientific ideas in a religiously compatible way. Other challenges were more difficult. Different religious traditions reacted in different ways, and even the same religious tradition could go through different phases at different times. The complexity continues to the present day.

A couple of general difficulties become immediately apparent:

- The Challenge to Design: Darwin's theory apparently eliminates design and purpose from creation. Also, violence, tragedy and death are part of the process. How can a loving God use cruelty and competition as a mechanism of creation?

Questions
1. List the difficulties posed for religion by Darwin's theory of evolution.
2. Critically evaluate each difficulty with regard to the Christian tradition.

Resources for further study
See teacher's text on CD-Rom for further suggestions.

- The Challenge to the Bible: Darwin's theory contradicts the simple understanding of the biblical story of Adam and Eve, as well as the 'Creation of the world in seven days' in Genesis.

- The Challenge to Human Dignity: Darwin's theory demotes humanity from the position of crown of creation. Humanity is nothing special; it has just outlived or 'done down' its rivals.

This topic is also considered in **Section B, Christianity: Origins and Contemporary Expressions; Section C, World Religions** and **Section H, The Bible: Literature and Sacred Text.**

- The Challenge to Morality: Darwin's theory means that virtue and goodness have no value in human life. Unbridled competition is sanctioned by nature itself.

None of the various religious groups reacted in a simple way to the challenges presented by evolution. No religious group was, or is, totally monolithic (uniform and united). Different places, different decades and different people ensured that there was plenty of variety in the religious response to evolution, even within the same denomination. Nevertheless, there were typical responses.

ANGLICAN REACTION

Evolutionary debates in Anglican circles produced at least as much compromise as confrontation. In England, the issue was confused with social and political struggles. No one was comfortable with a totally purposeless universe. Everyone wanted good to win in the end. Religious people wanted God to redeem the world. Secularists wanted a better life for the people.

Anglicans had to deal with the implications of an animal origin for humankind. Most held on to some divine intervention. Most Anglican theologians tended to a Lamarckian theory, or what one might call a 'designer brand' of evolution.

Anglicanism was greatly influenced by William Paley and his 'Watchmaker' argument, which emphasised God's transcendence. **Transcendence** (the quality of passing beyond) means that God is separate from the world of creation.

Evolution placed God's immanence in the foreground. **Immanence** (the quality of dwelling within) meant that God is to be found in the processes of creation. The immanence of God, of course, does not identify God with the universe; that is, it does not make both God and the universe the same. That is **pantheism** – the doctrine that everything is God.

Assignment

Summarise the Anglican reaction to Darwin's theory at the time of its development.

85

CATHOLIC REACTION

An Englishman, St George Mivart, formulated what came to be the classic Catholic position on evolution. He argued that there is nothing in Christian tradition that contradicts an evolutionary creative process by God. The creation of the human soul is the exception.

Catholics agree with evolution where the human body is concerned, but they insist on the special creation of the individual human soul, necessary to protect the dignity and value of the person. A creative intervention by God is required to bring each individual soul into existence.

Teilhard de Chardin

Teilhard de Chardin (1881-1955), a French Jesuit, scientist, philosopher and poet, tried to reconcile evolution with Christianity. He incurred much criticism from Catholic authorities. He said that evolution is heading for a God-given goal – an **Omega** point – of consciousness, at which the whole universe achieves integration. (*Omega* is the last letter of the Greek alphabet, a symbol of the goal of evolution.)

The challenge to the Bible was not as acute among Catholics as among some Protestants. (The Church had learned a stern lesson with Galileo.) The Pontifical Biblical Institute defended the literal interpretation of the book of Genesis in 1909, but critical approaches to the Bible were successfully assimilated into Catholic scholarship during the first half of the twentieth century.

Pope Pius XII

In 1950, evolution was declared an open question by Pope Pius XII in the encyclical *Humani Generis*. In 1996, Pope John Paul II pronounced evolution to be a well-established scientific theory. But Catholic teaching is always careful to state that the special creation of the human soul must be preserved.

FUNDAMENTALIST REACTION

The churches of the Reformation, which principally rely on the Bible alone for their religious authority, were challenged forcefully by evolutionary theory. Many of them hold to a strictly literal interpretation of the Bible. These churches are called **fundamentalist**.

Fundamentalists do not allow for metaphorical language or the 'accommodated sense' in the Bible narrative. They defend an instantaneous creation of fixed species, a special formation of the human being by God, and, maybe, an age of the earth that does not exceed six thousand years.

Assignments

1. Write a note on Catholic reaction to evolution. Research the role of Teilhard de Chardin in attempting to reconcile Catholicism with evolution theory.
2. Research the 'Scopes trial' in the US in 1925. What issues from that trial are still live in the US today?

86

The fundamentalist response to evolutionary teaching was very evident, especially in the United States, culminating in the famous 'Scopes Trial' or, as it became known to history, 'The Monkey Trial' in Tennessee in 1925. This approach is still alive today in the disputes over creationism in the American public schools.

GREGOR MENDEL (1822-1884)

Darwin's theory of evolution by natural selection did not explain two things: how random variation happened, and how inherited characteristics were transmitted between generations.

Gregor Mendel

A Moravian Augustinian monk, Gregor Mendel, began to supply both answers. His monastery conducted botanical research and Mendel spent years in the propagation of peas in the monastery garden. The significance of Mendel's observations and discoveries on the inherited characteristics of hybrids was unrecognised until thirty years after his death. Mendel's work laid the foundation for the science of modern genetics.

NEO-DARWINISM

Genetic mutation explains satisfactorily both variation and inheritance, thus explaining how Darwin's theory actually happens. This version of Darwinism is the modern consensus among biologists, zoologists, palaeontologists and all scientists working in the field of human and animal origins. 'Scientists agree that the evolutionary origin of animals and plants is a scientific conclusion beyond reasonable doubt,' says Francis Ayala. 'That evolution has occurred, in other words, is a fact.'

Genetics combined with natural selection comprises **neo-Darwinism** (New Darwinism). Neo-Darwinism poses a serious challenge to the Christian understanding of creation because it is very uncomfortable with any hint of purpose that dilutes randomness. Theologians are equally resistant to purposelessness. The question remains: in what way can design be admitted into the scientific account of human evolution? Or, put the other way, how far can the theological doctrine of creation accommodate chance? This remains particularly thorny ground for dialogue between science and religion.

Assignment

Write a note on the work of Gregor Mendel.

Questions

1. What two things did Darwin's theory of evolution *not* explain?
2. What is neo-Darwinism?
3. What particular challenge does neo-Darwinism pose to the Christian understanding of creation?

In summary...

Darwin had read Lyell and Malthus, collected a vast amount of fossils and observations of animals, reptiles and birds, and spent decades trying to make sense of how they developed. He already knew about Lamarckian evolution, in which acquired and purposeful characteristics were transmitted to descendants. Darwin's theory of evolution depends on random variations in situations of scarce resources conferring comparative advantage, which leads to the survival of the fittest, and sometimes emerges in the generation of new species. When applied to humanity, evolution excited controversy among Christian Churches, depending on how strictly literal were their respective interpretations of the Bible. Evolution challenges God's design, God's mercy, human dignity and morality and the interpretation of the Creation story in Genesis. Mendel's discovery of genetic inheritance of attributes, combined with classic Darwinism, constitutes Neo-Darwinian theory.

Chapter 7

Creation of the World (Science and Religion in Dialogue)

'To be or not to be: that is the question.'

Shakespeare, *Hamlet*

Resources for further study
See teacher's text on CD-Rom for further suggestions.

In this chapter you will learn about...

...the understanding of creation and God's action in the world in Christian teaching. Christian teaching is contrasted with Muslim teaching on creation. The contemporary ecological crisis poses a challenge for religion and science. The ideas of Thomas Berry, a theologian, are explained, and the Gaia theory of James Lovelock, a scientist, is outlined.

This topic is also considered in **Section A, The Search for Meaning and Values; Section B, Christianity: Origins and Contemporary Expressions** and **Section C, World Religions**.

CREATION IN CHRISTIANITY

THE QUESTION OF CREATION

'To be or not to be: that is the question.' William Shakespeare put that thought into Hamlet's head at a key moment of his famous play. It certainly is the question, for each of us and for the whole universe. Why is it that we exist? Why does the world exist, rather than not exist? The fact that anybody and anything exists is a great mystery.

Gottfried Wilhelm Leibnitz

'Why is there something rather than nothing?' is the way that Leibnitz (1646-1716), a German philosopher, posed this question. He argued that everything in the world requires a reason for its existence, since nothing happens without a reason. This is called the **principle of sufficient reason**. So, the world as a whole requires an explanation because it might not have existed at all, or it might have been very different. The only sufficient explanation for there being something rather than nothing, is God. God accounts for the existence, order and character of the entire universe. We say that God is the **Creator** of the universe.

CREATION AND ORIGIN

The next time you hear a discussion about God and creation, apply this very simple test. Just listen. Are they talking about something that happened many billions of years ago, at the beginning of time? Or are they referring to something that is going on now? They may say 'creation' but they may mean two quite different things. The first thing is the **origin of the universe**. The second thing is the **creation of the world**.

There is a very important distinction between the scientific question of the origin of the universe (How did the universe begin?) and the theological question of the creation of the world (Why is there something rather than nothing at all?). These are two fundamentally different questions and they require two quite separate answers. Science asks *how* things came about; theology asks *why* things came about. Science tells us the process of the beginning and development of the world; theology gives us the reason for the world's existence. And different religions and philosophies give different explanations for creation.

ETERNITY OF MATTER

'It all goes back to the Greeks.' Michael Constantine, a character in the film *My Big Fat Greek Wedding*, says this all the time. He is very funny, but he is quite correct. The Greeks, a long time ago, gave much thought to many things. The Greeks began many of the ways in which we think in European culture today.

Questions
1. What is the 'principle of sufficient reason'?
2. What do we mean when we say God is the 'Creator of the universe'?
3. What is the difference between scientific and theological approaches to the origin of the universe?

Fallen columns at the base of the ruins of the temple of Zeus in Ancient Olympia, Greece

Before the Christian era, many ancient Greek thinkers believed that matter was eternal and that God, in creating the world, had only put shape on already existing raw material. God had made a universe out of the chaos that existed previously.

Parmenides (540-480 BCE) taught that everything that exists in the world had always existed; it had no beginning and would have no end. This posed a problem for early Christians, who believed that God creates everything that exists, and everything that God creates is good. Only God is eternal; God always was and always will be. Christians knew that the universe was not eternal, because the Bible speaks of creation 'in the beginning'. Therefore, matter was not eternal. For Christians, if matter exists eternally alongside God, then God cannot be the Creator of everything. If matter is eternal and not created by God, then God is not sovereign and all-powerful, given that there are now two equal and eternal principles, matter and God.

CREATION IN THE BIBLE

The Bible teaches that 'in the beginning...God created the heavens and the earth' (Genesis 1:1). The whole universe and everything in it is created by God's word alone and 'God saw everything that he had made and, indeed, it was very good' (Genesis 1:31). Creation is the free act of God's love in bringing into being something other than God.

The biblical teaching on creation insists that the natural world is not divine. Many in the ancient world thought that the sun, the moon, the planets and the stars were gods. The Bible says that they are all God's creatures and depend on God.

This topic is also considered in Section G, Worship, Prayer and Ritual; Section H, The Bible: Literature and Sacred Text and Section I, Religion: The Irish Experience.

The biblical story states that the world is not a chaotic mess; the world is structured and ordered. God's goodness, wisdom and beauty is reflected, even if dimly, in creation. We see the glory of God in the beauty of the universe, as a work of art reflects the talent of the artist. 'The heavens are telling the glory of God' (Psalm 19).

Beehive huts on Skellig Michael, County Kerry

CREATION IN CELTIC CHRISTIANITY

Our Celtic Christian ancestors also saw the beauty of the natural world as a window into its Creator, as 'sacramental'. God's creation acts as a signpost to a greater mystery, the personal God who loves creation. Celtic Christians delighted in the wild, elemental, uncontrollable forces of nature as powerful witnesses to the limitless power of God. Celtic monasteries were built in remote parts of Ireland to be close to nature. St Kevin of Glendalough, and other saints, lived a life of simplicity in close harmony with the God-given state of nature. Celtic Christians felt overwhelmed by the presence of God in nature. Animals, birds, plants and running streams were all seen as praising the Creator and hinted at the greater glory of God. A ninth-century poem sums it up:

> Almighty Creator, who has made all things,
> The world cannot express all your glories,
> Even if the grass and the trees were to sing.

CHRISTIAN TEACHING ON CREATION

The Christian doctrine of *creatio ex nihilo* (Latin for 'creation out of nothing') counteracted Greek pagan ideas on the eternity of matter. God creates the world out of nothing. God does not use any pre-existing material. 'Out of nothing' is a difficult idea: it means 'not out of anything'.

Creation out of nothing or **creatio ex nihilo** makes a clear distinction between the Creator and creation. God is free to create the universe, but God is also free not to create it, or to create a different kind of universe. So the created universe is called **contingent**, meaning it need not exist, and it may in the future cease to exist. 'Contingent' means that the universe is not **necessary**; it does not 'have to be'.

Continuing creation or **creatio continua** means that God's work continues throughout the entire existence of the world. It is not confined to the first moments of existence. When we look at things around us, nothing can account for their existence. Each is contingent; it does not have to be. A contingent world means that everything is dependent on the creating and sustaining power of God. The work of the Creator continues through the natural processes of evolution, which are expressions of God's will. God, of course, is not the same as any other natural cause and God cannot be used to explain what cannot be explained scientifically at any given time.

DEIST CREATION

To see what this means, let us compare it with the deist view of creation. For **deism**, God is the designer and creator of the universe, but God is located outside what God has made. The world is like a machine, which God creates in the beginning, but afterwards it runs perfectly well on its own without the presence of God.

For Christians, this will not do. God is not like someone who builds a house and then goes away, leaving the house to stand on its own. God cannot be outside or absent from the world. How could we know anything about an absent God? God is powerfully present in creation, now and at all times. If God were not sustaining it, then it would cease to exist. So the universe is entirely dependent on God, not only in the past but also right now, for its continued existence.

Assignments

1. Summarise the biblical teaching on creation.
2. Write a note on creation in Celtic Christianity.
3. Explain what you understand by
   (a) creation out of nothing';
   (b) 'continuing creation'.

(*The topics from here to page 97 are also relevant for syllabus topic 1:1, which is dealt with in Chapter 2 of this text.*)

This topic is also considered in **Section A, The Search for Meaning and Values**.

Christian **theism** sums up the doctrine of creation by saying that God is both present in the world, and yet is greater than and different from the world: God is the 'beyond in our midst'. Two theological terms sum up this teaching: God is both **transcendent** and **immanent**. Theists believe in a personal God who is present in (immanent) but other than (transcendent) the world. The Bible says: 'The Lord is God in heaven above [transcendent] and on the earth beneath [immanent]; there is no other' (Deuteronomy 4:39).

Pompey the Great

When Pompey the Great, the all-conquering Roman general, captured Jerusalem in 63 BCE, he strode into the Temple. To the horror of the Jews, he directed his steps through the curtain veil into the Holy of Holies, the presence of God, the most sacred room into which the high priest could enter only on one day in the year. Pompey was surprised with what he found. What do you think it was?

Nothing. There was no statue, idol, image, icon or any other representation of God. This was to show that God, the Creator of the Universe, could not be identified with anything that God has made. God is transcendent.

Transcendence comes from the Latin, meaning 'to go beyond'. Transcendence is the claim that God is 'other than', totally different from the world God has made. There is a great gap between the Creator and the creation. On the other hand, creation is independent of, but not separate from, the Creator. Immanence comes from the Latin, meaning 'to dwell in', the claim that God is not separate from the world but is present in it. Creation is in a close relationship with God, yet it is free to be itself.

GOD'S ACTION

Question

Explain the following terms in your own words: Deism, Theism, Transcendence, Immanence.

How does God act in the world? If God creates the world, and if God participates in the ongoing development of the universe, and if God shares in the unfolding of the history of human endeavour, how can we understand God's action? Does God intervene, or interfere, or interrupt the normal course of nature? What is the relation between God's action and the natural causes of the universe?

The answer given by atheism is obvious: only the world exists; there are no causes that are not inside the universe; there is no God, and so there can be no intervention by God in the world.

The answer given by deism is also easy: God did create the world, but that was a long time ago; ever since, God has left the universe to get on by itself; since the beginning, God was not needed to interfere in the workings of the world, so there is no intervention by God in the world now.

The question then is: how does theism explain the action of God in the world?

GOD OF THE GAPS

One way of understanding the relationship of God to the universe is that God does those things that science cannot explain. So, if science can trace the entire line of human and animal evolution right back to the dawn of life, but cannot tell where life comes from, then God created life. If science can follow the development of the entire universe from the present moment back through thirteen or so billion years to the 'Big Bang', but cannot tell what happened before the 'Big Bang', then God is responsible for causing the 'Big Bang'. If science explains everything about the universe by probability, then God is responsible for the operation of chance. Whatever science cannot explain, God fills the gap.

Resources for further study
See teacher's text on CD-Rom for further suggestions.

This way of thinking is called the **'God of the Gaps'**. It means that god is used only to fill the gaps left by scientific ignorance. It is a very bad way of thinking, both scientifically and theologically. It is bad thinking scientifically because it labels as a divine mystery something that science cannot explain, instead of encouraging scientists to try to solve the puzzle. It is bad theologically, because it equates God's action to the kind of action available in nature; in other words, making God the same as any other natural cause. Finally, what happens to theology when scientists are eventually able to explain some of the gaps?

THE CHRISTIAN UNDERSTANDING OF CREATION

The traditional Christian way of understanding the action of God in the world is classically expressed by St Thomas Aquinas. God is the **First Cause**; everything else is a **Secondary Cause**. God is not a cause in the same way that things in the universe cause one another. God is transcendent; that is, completely different from the universe itself. We have no need to seek a spot, a particular location, or record a specific time, for God's creative action. God does not turn up in the universe, just at the beginning, nor at the end, nor anywhere in between. God is not part of the universe in any way at all.

In fact, God is not part of anything that exists. Every thing in the universe is caused by other things in the universe. Nothing

Assignment

What do you understand by the 'God of the Gaps'? Is such a notion relevant today? What modern versions of the 'God of the Gaps' can you recall? Is there a 'God of the Gaps' in your life?

This line of thinking that all things have two causes ('First Cause' and 'Secondary Cause') turns on the two meanings of 'is'. A thing can 'be' something ('the cat is black'), and it can just 'be' ('the cat is'). In English, this distinction is difficult to make. It is easier in Irish. What about other languages? What does it mean? When the Soviet cosmonauts first made it into space, Premier Khruschev boasted that they found no trace of God. What would you say in response to Nikita Khruschev? Write a letter to him.

This topic is also considered in **Section C, World Religions**.

explains totally the existence of anything. When we find a cause that does not depend on any other cause, that Cause we call 'God'. All beings have two causes. The Secondary Cause explains 'all' that a thing is; the First Cause explains that it 'is' at all. God is the First Cause of everything, but God works through Secondary Causes, laws of nature, human agency, random probability, evolutionary processes, subatomic events and so on. Secondary causes are what science studies.

CREATION IN ISLAM

Islam is the third of the great monotheistic (one God) religions that begin with Judaism and continue in Christianity. The basic principle of Islam is 'one-ness'. The central teaching of Islam is that God is one. The creed of Islam states: 'There is no God but Allah, and Muhammad is his prophet.' (*Allah* is the Arabic word for 'God'.)

According to Islam, God is the Creator of the universe. God creates because God is good (Allah the Beneficent). God freely creates this particular world, with its unique character and laws. Everything God creates is exactly as God wishes it to be, so the whole creation fits together in a meaningful way.

Creation is therefore sacred. The prophet Muhammad said, 'The whole of this earth is a mosque'; that is, the world is a place of worship of God the Creator.

ALLAH THE TRANSCENDENT

Islam believes that God brought the whole world into existence out of nothing. Everything is completely dependent upon God for its existence. The story of creation in the Qur'an (the sacred scripture of Islam) is very similar to the story of creation in Genesis. The heavens and the earth were created in six days, after which God withdrew to the throne from where God judges the world. So far, Islam and Judaism and Christianity agree.

Islam differs from Judaism and Christianity by not thinking of God as immanent to creation. In the Bible, God continues to interact with creation, taking an interest in history, and offering a covenant or agreement with a particular nation to be God's people. The choice of a particular people is central to biblical revelation, but foreign to the Qur'an. For Islam, all of humanity relate equally to God.

Islam stresses the transcendence of God and the gap between God and God's creatures. God is utterly different from the things God has created, including human beings. God is so transcendent that the Qur'an warns against connecting any creature with God. That is why Muslims regard Jesus as a great prophet, but they do not believe that Jesus is divine.

Detail from the Qu'ran

ISLAM AND SCIENCE

For this reason, too, Islam has a different relationship with science than has Christianity. For Muslims, the Book of God's Word is superior to the Book of the World. While Western science is secular and autonomous, Muslim science is subordinate to the revealed word of Allah in the Qur'an. If there is a contradiction between science and the Qur'an, then science is wrong. For example, Darwin's theory of evolution is a real obstacle in Muslim thought because it appears to exclude Allah's creation and contradicts the Qur'an.

Science in the Middle Ages was much more advanced in the Muslim Near East, than in Christian Europe. Muslim scholars preserved much of ancient learning in translation, and Muslim scientists made important advances in many of the sciences. For example, we still use what we call 'Arabic numerals', and refer to algebra and algorithms, both Arabic terms. The revival of learning in the West, the Renaissance, received much of its impetus from the Muslim world. Muslim scientists believe that the task of human intelligence is always to find out about Allah, the one Creator, and about Allah's creation. Therefore, there can be no conflict between the word of Allah and science.

ALLAH AND THE WORLD

Islam is not only a set of beliefs: it is also a way of life and it embodies a strong ethical attitude towards the world. There are practical moral demands made on the good Muslim to respect God's creation. Islam acknowledges that human beings are not the only creatures worthy of cherishing and protecting. God loves all creatures and has given us guidance as to how we should treat them.

Islam seeks to promote the material as well as the spiritual welfare of people. Technology is good as it brings benefits and relief from toil and drudgery, but it can also be harmful and damaging to the world if it is misused.

DUTY OF THE KHALIFAH

The right way for human beings to relate to the world is called *Khalifah* (from the Arabic meaning 'vice-regent'; this word is often rendered in English as 'Caliph'). God wants human beings to behave as God's representatives on earth; they must not exploit or pollute the planet, nor treat living things with contempt. The Qur'an speaks frequently of the need to keep the balance of nature and not to upset it.

God gives guidance to enable people to distinguish harmful and forbidden actions – because they are destructive and an offence to God – from those that are good and approved by God. All people will be called to give an account of their stewardship to God at the Last Judgement. God will judge people on how they have conducted themselves in the world, especially on the active kindness that is expected to all of God's creatures.

CREATION AND ECOLOGY

ECOLOGY

Ecology concerns the relationship between the human race and the world that we inhabit. The word comes from the Greek root word *oikos*, meaning 'home', and refers to the earth, our planet.

Assignments

1. Outline the understanding of creation in Islam.
2. How does the Islamic understanding of creation compare and contrast with the Christian understanding? (Higher Level)

This topic is also considered in Section F, Issues of Justice and Peace.

Resources for further study
See teacher's text on CD-Rom for further suggestions.

Ecology is the study of the complex conditions necessary for the surviving and thriving of all living things on our planet. Ecologically minded people are concerned with preserving the beauty of the natural world and the variety and diversity of living species on the earth, and the responsible use of the resources of the planet.

All is not well in the garden...

The view of planet Earth from space still evokes a sense of wonder. We gaze in awe at the deep blue beauty of the oceans, the rainforest green and the atmospheric white rain-bearing clouds. All testify that our planet is like a tiny garden alive with myriad life-forms in the immensity of dark space and dead planets. As far as we know, our planet is the only one in the vast universe capable of supporting life.

All is not well in the garden. This garden of ours is very fragile and is under threat from the most powerful living species, human beings. Ecologists today are agreed that we are not looking after or managing our planet properly. The delicate balance between all living things in their environment has been upset, so much so that we are now living through one of the greatest problems facing the world-wide community today: the ecological crisis.

ECOLOGICAL CRISIS

The **ecological crisis** refers to the breakdown in the web of relationships among living things and the earth environment. It raises ethical questions about the way human beings are contributing to the crisis: for example, burning rainforests, depleting the ozone layer, global warming, polluting air, water and soil, and eliminating rare species. People are increasingly worried about the way the natural world is being destroyed.

Pope John Paul II summed up the dismay: 'We begin to ask how we have destroyed so much. We also ask anxiously, if it is possible to remedy the damage which has already been done.' The United Nations also has often spoken out on the need for environmental protection, emphasising that the resources of our planet, on which we depend for life, have a claim on our concern and protection.

The ecological crisis is a great area for debate between science and religion. Who or what is responsible for the ecological crisis? Both religion and science are charged with contributing in different ways to the crisis.

There are two views of science and technology and of their impact on the environment. There is, first of all, the good view. Many people are happy about science and technology because they have very effectively used the natural world in the name of economic progress. Science and technology have changed our world for the better.

Then there is the bad view. Science and technology are blamed for environmental abuse. There is a price to pay for prosperity and progress: draining the earth's non-renewable resources and polluting our planet. Nature has no defence against the disruptive powers of human beings.

Both views raise questions about the moral values we live by and how we use science and technology. The point is not that science is bad in itself, but that human beings, institutions and nations can misuse it for selfish reasons.

THE CARTESIAN SPLIT

This topic is also considered in **Section A, The Search for Meaning and Values; Section F, Issues of Justice and Peace** and **Section I, Religion: The Irish Experience.**

The reason can be traced back to the Enlightenment. As we have seen, René Descartes taught that there are two basic kinds of being: the objective natural world 'out there' and the subject, me, 'in here'. Cartesian dualism divided mind (thinking things) from matter (material things). Human beings felt free to manipulate the world 'out there', because it was so separate from us.

Just as mind and matter were divided, so were religion and science. The Cartesian Split was to lead to the deist view that God is entirely remote from the world, which has been left to run by itself according to the laws of physics. God is no longer seen as involved in the operation of the world, another reason for treating nature as the plaything of humans.

The elimination of a religious dimension from nature has led to its violation, and scientific materialism has filled the void. If the natural world is just physical forces, without spiritual or moral value, then it is without meaning and purpose. The only reason for environmental concern has to do with its usefulness for humans. Without the recovery of a religious vision, humans will continue to destroy the planet.

Have Christians themselves exploited the natural world? Religion is accused of contributing to the ecological crisis because it neglects the natural world in its teachings. Religious texts appear to say almost nothing in favour of promoting care for the earth. Religions can be too 'otherworldly'. This world is not our real home; our real home, they say, is in heaven.

THOMAS BERRY

An American monk and theologian, Thomas Berry is very critical of his own Christian tradition. He traces the roots of the ecological crisis today to 'prophetic religion'. He thinks the Bible has always looked toward a future messianic age and that this has released a drive toward 'progress' that is draining the earth of its resources.

Thomas Berry thinks that we need a New Story of the Universe. Our universe is embarked on a restless adventure, he says, and we are part of this journey. Our universe has unfolded slowly in a thirteen-billion-year story of adventurous wandering. The story of a great cosmic evolutionary process of increasing complexity reaches a level of awareness in human beings. We need this new story, which would enable the religions of the world to have a new relationship to the universe.

He feels that the Bible stories do not connect us to the natural world anymore, that nature has disappeared from Christian teaching, that the Book of Nature has been closed to us. Thomas Berry says: 'Becoming literate with printed books, we become illiterate in the great book of the universe.' The effect has been the detachment of the natural world from the Bible story of God's saving love for humans.

So Berry proposes that 'the journey story of the Bible needs retelling within the larger context as the journey of the universe'. The fate of humanity is bound up with the fate of the planet. We have to be reconciled with nature and not dominate it.

This begins a debate about environmental abuse and the lack of Christian response to these pressing problems. Thomas Berry has raised the important question: can Christianity help us in discovering an ecological ethic?; that is, the proper relationship that should exist between humans and the environment.

BASIS OF CHRISTIAN ECOLOGY

What has Christianity to offer to the ecological debate? Christianity can provide a vision that would support an ecological ethic; that is, a vision of the world as God intended it to be.

Questions

1. What do you understand by ecology?
2. What is the 'ecological crisis'?
3. How does science contribute to this crisis?
4. How does religion contribute to this crisis?

Thomas Berry

The Bible views creation as God's possession, not ours. God entrusted the gift of nature to the safekeeping of human beings. Human beings are created in the **image of God**. That means that they have a purpose: to be God's representatives to the natural world in a relationship of partnership. We are accountable to God for our actions because we are free and morally responsible.

Since God gives and sustains life, the Bible demands that we imitate God in sustaining life on earth. Humanity is charged with tending creation, as Adam was entrusted with Eden, to work it and take care of it (Genesis 2:15).

STEWARDS OF CREATION

We are the earth's trustees. A trustee is someone to whom something valuable is entrusted in safekeeping for the benefit of others. Humans are not the owners of the earth but trustees who act in God's name. The proper management of the earth's resources is a trusteeship for our children and for future generations. We are the stewards of creation.

This topic is also considered in **Section C, World Religions; Section G, Worship, Prayer and Ritual** and **Section I, Religion: The Irish Experience**.

There is no justification in the Bible for abusing the earth. Genesis encourages humans to 'subdue the earth'. This means the sensible use of technologies for the benefit of all peoples and of all life-forms on the planet.

Religious people, like our Celtic ancestors, see nature as 'sacramental'. Clean water, fertile soil, clear skies, bright light, thunder and rain communicate the reality of the sacred. The natural world is a signpost pointing, however distantly, to its Creator. Gerard Manley Hopkins wrote: 'The world is charged with the grandeur of God.' So nature is worth saving, not because it is divine, but because it is sacramental, showing us something of the hidden mystery of God.

A NEW CREATION

The Bible is very much concerned with the future of creation; it looks forward to a 'new creation', 'a new heaven and a new earth' (Revelation 21:1). If we are convinced that the earth has a future, we will want to care for it. Our actions have eternal significance. So the care for God's creation plays an important role in the light of the future renewal of the earth, when God's kingdom finally comes.

St Francis of Assisi, who was renowned for his love of nature

God creates, sustains and empowers the universe and will bring it to completion in the future. Christianity gives us reasons to respect the integrity of creation, the urgency to undo the damage already done and the moral impetus to preserve the environment for the future. Science gives us amazing detailed facts about the natural world, but science cannot give us values. Religious beliefs about right and wrong provide us with moral values. The Christian vision is that both universe and humans exist for God.

The Enlightenment Age thought about the natural world as a machine. A more ancient view thought about the earth as something alive; it thought that the world is an organism. A contemporary version of this latter view suggests that it is a superior way to see nature, providing us with a better response to the ecological crisis.

JAMES LOVELOCK

In the 1970s, the scientist James Lovelock proposed the **Earth System hypothesis** that the whole planet behaves as if it were alive, correcting its conditions to suit the emergence and survival of life-forms on it. Lovelock was drawing attention to the remarkably self-adjusting conditions of our earth, which dead planets, like Mars, lack. The earth's capacity to repair, regulate and renew itself makes it more like an organism than a machine.

The presence of life has changed the planet, giving rise to self-regulating mechanisms that allow life to continue. Life does not simply adapt to its environment but, in fact, shapes the environment to its own advantage. Living organisms continually renew and regulate the chemical balance of air, water and soil, keeping the environmental conditions stable, within certain ranges. For example, the oxygen level of the atmosphere is delicately balanced at about 21 per cent. A little more, and fires would break out all over the place; a little less, and air-breathing creatures like us would die.

THE GAIA HYPOTHESIS

James Lovelock explained his idea to a neighbour, who happened to be the teacher and writer William Golding, author of *Lord of the Flies*. Golding told him that the phrase 'Earth System' did not catch the imagination. Why, he suggested, do you not call it the Gaia hypothesis, after the ancient Greek Mother Goddess of the earth? And so the **Gaia hypothesis** was born.

Many scientists reject Gaia as a scientific theory. Environmentalists disagree with Gaia as a living, self-regulating earth. Others say that the metaphor of a living planet has been pushed too far. Some theologians think that the mixture of scientific with religious claims, personifying the earth as a mystical agent, like a Mother Goddess, brings to

Questions

1. Can you point to examples today where human injustice or wrongdoing has resulted in ecological damage?
2. Do you think that what people believe as well as how they live affects the well-being of the created world?
3. What is humanity's responsibility before God with regard to the natural world?
4. How do you understand the idea that humans are made 'in the image of God'?

James Lovelock

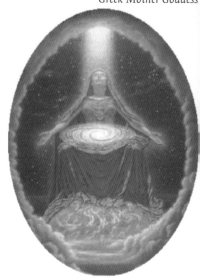

Depiction of Gaia, the ancient Greek Mother Goddess

Questions

1. Explain the Earth System hypothesis.
2. How did the Gaia hypothesis evolve?
3. What is pantheism?

Assignments

1. Outline the contemporary ecological crisis.
2. Present the perspective of Thomas Berry, a theologian, on the crisis.
3. Present the perspective of James Lovelock, a scientist, on the crisis.

mind **pantheism** (the belief that the universe and everything in it is divine).

But the Gaia hypothesis is a useful metaphor for illustrating the scientific picture of our planet 'teeming with life' and the human abuse that threatens it. The image of the earth as alive may help us to respect its integrity and protect it, more than we would if we regard it as a machine.

Revision of Important Terms

Look up the following terms which you have come across in this chapter and briefly explain each one. Each of these terms is printed in bold in the text.

Principle of sufficient reason, Creator, Origin of the universe, Creation of the world, *Creatio ex nihilo*, Contingent/Necessary, *Creatio continua*, Deism, Theism, Transcendent, Immanent, 'God of the Gaps', First Cause, Secondary Cause, Ecology, Ecological crisis, Image of God, Earth System hypothesis, Gaia hypothesis, Pantheism.

In summary...

For Christians, creation is not explaining the origin of the universe, but explaining the fact that it exists at all. Christians believe God freely creates a universe from nothing. The 'God of the Gaps' says that God intervenes only at points that science cannot as yet explain.

Islam stresses the transcendence of God. Scientific knowledge is not as certain as revealed knowledge from the Qur'an.

The ecological crisis today poses the challenge to science of responsible technology, and to theology of neglecting the care of the earth. Thomas Berry claims that theology needs the New Story of stewardship. James Lovelock says that the earth is now past the 'tipping point' of global warming, and that responsible people, scientists, politicians and religious leaders should be alert to the radical new initiatives required to slow, halt, reverse or cope with the crisis before us.

Part 3: Current Issues for Religion and Science – Origins

Note: Students study *either*
Part Three *or* Part Four

Chapter 8

The New Cosmology
(The Debate about Origins)

'God saw everything that he had made,
and indeed, it was very good.'

Genesis 1:31

Resources for further study
See teacher's text on CD-Rom for
further suggestions.

This topic is also considered in
Section A, The Search for Meaning
and Values.

In this chapter you will learn...

*...to explore cosmology, the whole universe, its origins and its end.
Two ancient cosmologies (stories of the universe) are presented and
compared: the Babylonian and the one from the Bible. Then two
contemporary cosmologies are explained: the 'Big Bang' and the
'creationist' position.*

Take-off of Voyager I

THE QUESTION OF BEGINNINGS

OUR PLACE IN SPACE?

The **cosmos** (from the Greek word meaning
the ordered universe) is everything that
exists. **Cosmology** is the science of the
universe, its origins, its existence and its
destiny. It covers its story through time
from the very first moment to the very last
moment. So cosmology is about all the
space there is, and all the time there is,
because it is about everything that was, is or
will be.

The spacecraft *Voyager I* turned its camera
on the earth for the last time on 14 February
1990. It was heading for outer space. No
human being was on board, so there was
no thought of St Valentine's cards. But the
spacecraft still looked back and took a
picture of home. We could see ourselves
from four billion miles away. It is not a very
good photo because it was taken into the
sun; there is too much light shining
through the picture, and earth looks like a
pale blue dot...

Carl Sagan (1934-96) was a scientist who tried to make people understand the awe and wonder and sheer fascination of cosmology. He meditated on the photo of the pale blue dot and pondered on the fact that the whole of human history and destiny is contained in that pale blue dot. It looks so small in the vastness of space that it shows the foolishness of human pride.

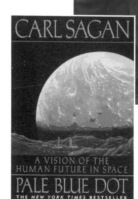

CURRENT DEBATES

THE EXPANDING UNIVERSE

THE UNIVERSE IS BIG...

How long is your arm? From shoulder to fingertips, it should be almost a metre long, if you are eighteen years old. A kilometre is 1,000 metres. The earth is 13,000 kilometres in diametre and 41,000 kilometres in circumference. The moon is 385,000 kilometres away from the earth and the sun is around 150,000,000 kilometres away. The nearest star is about 40,000,000,000,000 kilometres away from the earth.

Carl Sagan and (left) his book, 'Pale Blue Dot'

Things are very big. The nearest star is our cosmic neighbour in our village of stars. You can see our star-village any starry night. Look out for the 'Milky Way'. That cloud of stars running across the sky is the middle of our own star-village. In fact, that is how any star-village gets its name: **galaxy** (Greek *galaktos*, meaning milk). The 'Milky Way' galaxy contains a hundred billion stars and is an immense distance across.

Questions

1. What are your thoughts on the place of human beings in the universe?
2. Is Carl Sagan right? Are we a proud race?

The Milky Way

The Parsons Telescope at Birr,
County Offaly

William Parsons, the third Earl of Rosse, who lived in Birr, County Offaly, built a very large telescope at his castle in 1845. It was the largest telescope in the world for the next seventy years. With it, he first identified star-clusters or **nebulae** (Latin *nebula*, meaning cloud or vapour) as other galaxies outside the Milky Way. So we found many more star-villages and star-towns, and even cities of stars, other than our own. The universe was much larger than we could ever have imagined. You should go and see the Parsons Telescope, where these discoveries were made, on your next visit to Birr. It is located in the Irish National Historic Science Centre.

Today astronomers estimate that there are forty billion galaxies, many bigger than ours. So you now see why Carl Sagan says that there are more galaxies than people.

Assignment

The class might consider a visit to Birr and the Irish National Historic Science Centre in the context of an assignment on the universe and its size. An observatory nearer your school would also suffice. (List of observatories in teacher's text on CD-Rom.)

MEASURING SPACE AND TIME

The distances in space are unimaginably huge. They are so big that normal measures of length will not work. Instead of metres, or kilometres, astronomers use the **light year**, which is the distance that light travels in one year. Light is the fastest thing in the universe, and it always travels at the same speed, 300,000 kilometres a second.

Now. Work out how long a light year is in kilometres.

Your answer for the length of a light year in kilometres should be about 95 with eleven zeros after it. The nearest star is distant from us by 40 with twelve zeros in kilometres. So, travelling at the speed of light, it would take you four years to reach it. Or put it another way, the nearest star is four light years away.

(P.S. In the USA, a billion is a thousand million, or one with nine zeros after it. In the UK, a billion is a million million, or one with twelve zeros after it. We will use the USA convention. It is more fun because everything seems even bigger...!!)

LOOKING BACK IN TIME

What this means is astonishing. Light is the fastest thing possible. We cannot see anything unless light from it arrives at our eyes. Therefore, if something is so far away that it takes time for light to travel from there to here, we are looking at it as it was and where it was sometime in the past. For instance, we are seeing the sun as it was eight minutes ago. The nearest star looks to us as it was four years ago.

When we look at stars and galaxies millions and even billions of light years from earth, we are gazing right back into the past of the universe. Cosmologists say that the universe is only about thirteen or fourteen billion years in age (that is, in USA billions); so if we see something twelve billion light years away, we will be close to the start of everything.

So far, telescopes have penetrated about twelve billion light years into cosmic space, or twelve billion light years back in the universe's history, whichever way you want to think about it. We are almost at the limits of the visible universe because, before the formation of galaxies and stars, there was no light at all; matter was dark – so we will not be able to see it. Those were the truly Dark Ages.

THE UNIVERSE IS GETTING BIGGER...

Have you ever stood beside a railway track and listened to the screech of the train's whistle? Or by the side of the road as an ambulance, with its siren on, came by? As it is coming toward you, you hear a high pitch, but as it passes you, the pitch changes immediately to a lower pitch. This is called the **Doppler effect** and has to do with the frequency of sound as the source approaches you or recedes from you.

A similar effect occurs with light. As the source of light moves away from you, the frequency of the light will move through the colours of the rainbow from violet to red. This is called the **red shift** on the spectrum. By using this property of light, astronomers determined that the galaxies around us are all moving away from one another like spots on a balloon being inflated. The universe is expanding rapidly in all directions.

The scientist who discovered that we live in an expanding universe was Edwin Hubble, after whom the orbiting space telescope is named, and he made this discovery in 1929.

Edwin Hubble

BIG CHILL OR BIG CRUNCH?

So we find that we are living in a universe that is getting bigger and bigger at an enormous speed. How long can this go on? It looks as if the universe will not last for ever. What will be the fate of the universe? One of two things will probably happen.

In the first scenario, the galaxies 'thin out' as the universe expands much more slowly and gets cooler, and the vast energy of the universe dissipates. This process is called **entropy**. We are familiar with the fact that eventually all things cool off and fall apart. That happens to the cosmos too. The stars dim and eventually go out. The temperature reaches

Questions

1. What is a galaxy?
2. What do you understand by 'a light year'?
3. What is the difference between the 'Big Chill' and the 'Big Crunch'?
4. How do we know that the universe is getting bigger?

Assignment

The previous section showed how small the human race is when compared to the size and age of the universe. Now the universe itself seems to be a wasteland of arbitrary forces, rushing apart and charging together, in a purposeless pulse of energy.

We are like microbes clinging to an apple hanging from a tree in an orchard on an island in an ocean. Does what is going on 'out there' have any possible meaning for us?

Resources for further study
See teacher's text on CD-Rom for further suggestions.

absolute zero, minus 273 degrees centigrade. There will be a long cosmic night. Cosmologists refer to this as the 'Big Chill'.

In the alternative, the expansion comes to a stop. Then the gravity of all the matter in the universe starts to drag everything together. The universe contracts rapidly, in the same way that it expanded, and, of course, it heats up. Eventually, all the galaxies in the universe smash together and everything collapses into a very small pellet. The universe then will be infinitely dense, infinitely small, and infinitely hot, ready, perhaps, for another 'Big Bang'. Astronomers refer to this as the 'Big Crunch'.

Robert Frost wrote about these alternatives in his poem 'Fire and Ice':

> Some say the world will end in fire,
> Some say in ice.
> From what I've tasted of desire
> I hold with those who favour fire.
> But if it had to perish twice,
> I think I know enough of hate
> To say that for destruction ice
> Is also great
> And would suffice.

How much time have we got? Well, if the universe is heading for a Big Chill, we have over 150 billion years to prepare. If, on the other hand, we are doomed to the Big Crunch, we could have as little as ten to twenty billion years more. So we need not be worried about the fate of the universe for the moment. At least, not before the end of the term!

THE ANTHROPIC UNIVERSE

THINGS ARE MEANT...

The Expanding Universe poses a challenge of meaning. How can the human race and planet Earth have any importance in the whole scheme of things if everything is so vast and the process so unsympathetic? How can the universe itself be purposeful and meaningful if it is destined inevitably either to explode or collapse? How can there be purpose to anything? Are things meant to be as they are?

THE SPECTATORS IN THE GRANDSTAND

Imagine that you are a marathon runner. For over twenty-six miles, you have been running through city streets. Then you swing down a ramp leading under a very large round building through a tunnel in the cool dark. You charge up the slope and burst into the sunlight.

You are on an orange clay running-track. Towering above is a multi-level stadium. For this is the Olympic Games and you are the leading runner in the marathon race, the last event on the last afternoon of the last day of competition.

PEOPLE ARE MEANT...

These sports fans are meant to be here. These spectators did not happen by chance. That is a picture of the universe. Spectators are meant to be here. We are the crowd in the stadium. The race is meant for us. This idea is called the anthropic principle.

For discussion

1. Are you sometimes aware of meaning in apparently purposeless events?
2. Does the belief that 'things are meant' make any sense to you?

Freeman Dyson

THE ANTHROPIC PRINCIPLE

The **anthropic principle** states that the universe is meant to contain intelligent life that is able to understand it. (*Anthropos* is the Greek word for man or human.) Freeman Dyson, Emeritus Professor of Physics at the Institute for Advanced Study in Princeton, New Jersey, says that the universe is expecting us.

We have discovered that we are puny but intelligent beings in a huge, mindless and careless universe. This suggested to many scientists in the past, and to some today, that humanity is the product of a chance process. Instead of being the centre and purpose of everything, as the medieval people believed they were, these scientists believe that there is no centre and no purpose anywhere for anybody.

But this same situation suggests to other scientists and cosmologists that the universe is in some way meant for the emergence of intelligent life. This becomes apparent when we consider the rarity of conscious intelligence in the universe, and the very long odds of its evolution if we rely on chance alone for an explanation. The human brain is, by far, the most evolved and most complex and most wonderful thing in the universe. Not the biggest, nor the brightest, nor the fastest, but the most amazing.

In other words, the universe is a stadium, and the earth is the grandstand, and we are the spectators. And we are also the runners!

FINE-TUNING THE UNIVERSE

Have you ever gone to a concert or musical early? As you sit in your seat, waiting for the show to commence, the musicians spend the time plucking at their violin strings, adjusting their bows, taking notes from the piano and playing short bursts of music. What they are doing is making sure that their instruments are at concert pitch (meaning vibrating at a standard frequency so that they can all play in tune). This process is called **fine-tuning.**

The anthropic principle maintains that the universe is 'fine-tuned'. Everything in the universe relating to life is adjusted within such a narrow range of values that it appears to be the result of care, not chance. It looks more likely that things were meant from the beginning to be exactly the way they are.

If, for example, gravity were to be slightly stronger or slightly weaker, if the electron were slightly bigger or smaller, if the stars' energy were a little more or a little less, if the speed of the universe's expansion were a little quicker or a little slower, then life of any kind would be impossible. And the proportion by which any of the changes would throw the whole thing out of kilter is infinitesimal or, in other words, very small indeed. The universe is really fine-tuned.

There are at least three conclusions from these scientific considerations:
1. We must explain the 'fine-tuning' by invoking an intelligence outside the universe that arranged the process to be so precise.
2. We must explain 'fine-tuning' by saying that there are other universes outside this one, in which life did not evolve at all.
3. We have no need to explain 'fine-tuning', except to acknowledge that the emergence of life is, *before the fact*, a very long shot, but, *after the fact*, is, quite simply, the fact. (Think of this in terms of a rank outsider winning the Grand National!)

ANCIENT COSMOLOGIES

CONTRASTING PICTURES

We now turn to depictions of the universe, ancient and contemporary. There are two very **ancient cosmologies** (accounts of the world and the cosmos) that have played an important role throughout the ages in Western Christian civilisation. The first is the **Babylonian** cosmology from the Enuma Elish epic, and the other is its counterpart, as given in the **biblical** book of Genesis.

THE ENUMA ELISH

Read the Creation extract from the ancient Babylonian account of how the world began (available in teacher's text on CD-Rom). The Enuma Elish (Akkadian for 'when the sky', the first words of the epic) was written 1200 years before Christ, in the country now known as Iraq. It tells how Mesopotamia, the land of the two great rivers, became the home of the gods.

For discussion

What do you think of the anthropic principle and the idea that the earth is 'fine-tuned'? Is life meant to be? Are the events of your life meant to be?

Resources for further study
See teacher's text on CD-Rom for further suggestions.

Tiamat, the dragon goddess of chaos and darkness, is battled by Marduk, god of justice and light

Questions on the Enuma Elish

1. Can you make out the story in the extract from Enuma Elish? What happened? Who did what?
2. What does the story mean? What is the nature of the sea, the river, the land?
3. What is the nature of human beings? What is their function?
4. What is the nature of the gods? What is their function?
5. Which questions about the universe, about the human race, about history, about geography, about life in general, about the gods, would this story explain?
6. What kind of world does this story depict for us?
7. What is the basic theme of the story?

This topic is also considered in **Section A, The Search for Meaning and Values** and **Section H, The Bible: Literature and Sacred Text**.

The story ends with Marduk tearing up the body of Tiamat in order to make the world out of her blood and guts. The fight between the gods is the way creation happens. Good comes out of evil. But evil can come back...

The story of creation that emerges from the Enuma Elish is **from Chaos through Conflict to Cosmos.**

If you lived in the delta plain and salt marshes of southern Iraq, south of modern Baghdad, where the two great rivers of Mesopotamia flow into the Persian Gulf, you would understand how the rivers and the ocean, the sky and the land can at times be mixed up, as the water flows over the fields, as the earth heaves in earthquakes as though the dead god were coming back to life.

Even if you do not live in Iraq, you may easily believe that human beings are fated to serve the great ones of earth and heaven. Political life, then and now, is much the same – a story of exploitation and domination, of violence and conquest. History repeats itself. Only the names change.

You may also believe that the universe contains evil as well as good elements. You may even think that there are such beings as evil spirits, who are equal in power to the good spirits. And you may rely on superstitious practices to keep the evil powers in check.

THE BOOK OF GENESIS

The first chapter of the first book of the Bible begins 'In the beginning'... That supplies the name of the book: Genesis. (*Genesis* is the Greek word for beginning.) It was written about six hundred years before Jesus, and the scripture scholars guess that it was a priest who wrote it. This is because the author makes mention of festivities and other rituals.

Resources for further study
See teacher's text on CD-Rom for further suggestions.

Read the account of the first week of creation from Genesis, Chapter 1.

The priestly writer of Genesis is familiar with the main lines of the Enuma Elish story. We can conclude this from the specific contradictions between them.

For Genesis, there is no fight, no opposition, no other power. God has only to speak, and it happens immediately. The story of creation that the book of Genesis tells is **from Void through Word to World.** This is not the case in the Enuma Elish.

For Genesis, there is no mess, no destruction, no death. The Lord God of creation is a God of order. Every thing is in its place. Every thing is as it should be. Every being does as it should do. This is not true of the Enuma Elish.

Nothing is mixed up with anything else. The air is for birds, the sea for fish, the land for animals and human beings. The waters and the land are separated. This is clearly not so in the Enuma Elish.

So there is a contrast between the two accounts: the first (Enuma Elish) is based on conflict and the victory of good over evil; the second (Genesis) is the simple assertion of order and reason and good authority.

LESSONS FROM GENESIS

The writer of Genesis places the weekly holy day in the very first week of the world itself. There is, one might say, a Jewish joke here: 'What is so important that you have to work on Sunday? Are you making the universe?' God rested. So should everyone else, after the week's work.

A couple more insights from the Genesis account of creation are just as relevant today as in ancient times.

The world is good, everything in it is good, even sea monsters and serpents and things that crawl on the earth. Nothing that God made is bad.

Human beings have a special place and importance and dignity in the world. We are made in the image of God.

As the agents of God, we are meant to be creative ourselves, to understand the Word of God, and to take care of the earth.

TWO ACCOUNTS: BABYLONIAN AND HEBREW

Both accounts assume the same shape and plan of the universe. In both, the earth is flat and it is surrounded by a

Questions on the book of Genesis

1. Outline the biblical creation story in a few sentences.
2. How does the story differ from the Enuma Elish?
3. How would you guess that the author of Genesis knew something about the Enuma Elish?
4. Where does Genesis contradict the Enuma Elish?
5. Draw the plan of the world according to Genesis, and the plan of the world according to the Enuma Elish.

dome above, and by water on all sides, the four points of the compass, above and below.

It is a very static view of the universe: we have the sun, moon and stars moving across the dome; water sometimes encroaches on the land by coming down from above, or from the sides, or even, on occasion, from below, but apart from those, the earth is immovable and unchanging. There are no revolutions or orbits or spheres.

But the contrasting visions of life that the accounts portray are theological, religious and human rather than astronomical. Each conveys a relationship between the divine and the human that is quite different. Each expresses a destiny and a status for the human race that is totally different. Both have a similar picture of the universe, but different pictures of how men and women live in it.

The theme of the first account (Enuma Elish) is that human beings are the slaves of the gods and of the great ones on earth. Human beings are the lowest of the low. Human beings are nothing special. The universe is a product of violence and conflict. Some beings dominate others. Might is right.

Assignments

1. Explain the importance of reflecting on and studying origins.
2. Compare and contrast the Enuma Elish and Genesis accounts of the origin of the universe. Note the status of human beings in each.

The theme of the second account (Genesis) is that the universe is a product of the reason and wisdom of God. Every being should take care of the universe and the beings in it. We human beings have a special place in the universe. We human beings should thank God for the gift of life. We human beings should be able to rest, enjoy peace and bring joy to the world.

CONTEMPORARY COSMOLOGIES

Georges Lemaitre

Today there are many ways that scientists, cosmologists, astronomers, philosophers and theologians approach the study of the universe. We are going to examine two of them in some detail, to appreciate their differences and to assess how each implies a different theology, philosophy and attitude to life, to humanity and to the universe. The first is the standard modern cosmological account of the origin and structure of the universe, usually called the 'Big Bang' theory. The other is the doctrine of **creationism.**

GEORGES LEMAITRE (1894-1966)

By the 1920s, evidence was gathering that the universe was expanding, and cosmologists were agreed that this seemed to be the case. What was in dispute, however, was what had happened in the past.

A Belgian priest, Georges Lemaitre, proposed the 'hypothesis of the primeval atom'. He suggested that the universe had expanded from a very small beginning, a nucleus, which had exploded and expanded rapidly. Lemaitre's theory states that everything began with an immense explosion, from which emerged the entire physical universe.

Scientists at the time believed that the universe was eternal and unchanging. Albert Einstein did not like the idea of the primeval atom. For a true scientist, it smacked too closely of a religious idea. Lemaitre himself tried to keep science clear of theology, and concentrated on observations and calculations. The prominent scientist Fred Hoyle derided the primeval atom theory as 'The Big Bang'.

Assignment

Write a note on the 'Big Bang' theory from the 1920s to the present day.

Debate

In 1929, Edwin Hubble (1889-1953) discovered the red shift, showing that the universe was indeed expanding (see p. 108). Opinion changed. Most scientists now agreed that expansion happened, though some still did not believe in the initial explosion. These ones held the **'Steady State' theory.** But they had to show how matter in the cosmos remained the same in quantity even though it was expanding and thinning.

To solve this problem, Fred Hoyle (1915-2001) put forward the idea of **continuous creation**. This stated that new atoms of hydrogen came into existence to balance the expansion of the universe. It did not seem to require much creation: one atom of hydrogen per six thousand cubic metres of space every hundred thousand years would do the trick nicely.

Fred Hoyle

Observations in the 1960s settled the debate, for the moment anyway. Two Bell Laboratory scientists identified cosmic microwaves left over from the 'Big Bang' at the predicted frequency. Luckily, Georges Lemaitre heard about the confirmation of his theory just before he died in 1966.

Resources for further study
See teacher's text on CD-Rom for further suggestions.

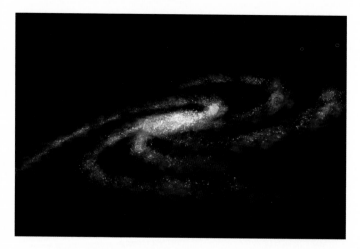

In the 1990s, various satellite telescopes revealed the cosmic microwaves in fascinating detail. Lemaitre's idea is now the only cosmological theory that is widely accepted among scientists, and Fred Hoyle's insult has become its proud label: the 'Big Bang' theory.

CREATIONISM

Creationism holds that God created the universe in seven days, as described in the first chapter of the book of Genesis. Strict creationism believes that the seven days are a literal week of twenty-four-hour days; progressive creationism allows that the biblical 'day' can stand for a very long period of time.

Recent variations include **'Old Earth' creationism**, which teaches that the universe is very ancient according to the geological record, though the different species were directly and unchangeably created by God, and **'New Earth' creationism**, which holds to a later creation of the universe within the last ten thousand years.

THE SCOPES TRIAL

Clarence Darrow and William Jennings Bryan at the Scopes Trial

In 1925, the State of Tennessee had enacted a law forbidding the teaching of evolution in public high schools. The Civil Liberties Union arranged a test case, with the co-operation of the town of Dayton, in which a teacher would be accused of teaching evolution. The town authorities were interested in publicity. Both the anti-evolutionary movement and the libertarians wanted to galvanise public opinion.

The teacher was John T. Scopes, a young science teacher and football coach, single, pleasant, popular and well thought of in the town. The prosecutor and advocate for creationism was William Jennings Bryan, a former presidential candidate. The defending lawyer was Clarence Darrow, a noted champion of progressive thought. For eight days (not seven) in 1925, the trial lasted. In the end, Scopes was convicted, but fined a dollar in punishment. The judge obviously did not take the 'crime' very seriously.

But evolutionists had a sample of rural bigotry, and a hero in Clarence Darrow. Creationists had a taste of media prejudice, and a hero in William Jennings Bryan. H.L. Mencken and all the journalists had plenty of satirical copy. Dayton, Tennessee, had a tourist bonanza. Everyone succeeded in what they wanted to accomplish.

The event, however, was more balanced, more ambiguous and more prophetic than the dramatic play by Lawrence and Lee, *Inherit the Wind* (or the film with Spencer Tracy, Frederic March and Gene Kelly), ever depicted.

CREATION SCIENCE

After the Scopes trial, anti-evolutionists turned to a new tactic. Instead of trying to exclude evolution from high school classrooms on religious grounds, they decided to include creationism on scientific grounds. They claim 'equal time' with evolution teaching, because they say that creationism is an alternative *scientific* account of the origin of the universe.

Creationist scholars engage in research projects, such as finding the ark of Noah, investigating the age of fossils, establishing the true geological record and so on. They are already convinced of the error of evolution, and do not accept any data that support it. Accordingly, their science is questionable and their credentials suspect. This is because they are not sufficiently open-minded to what science may discover.

INTELLIGENT DESIGN

More recently, there has been debate in USA education circles about '**intelligent design**'. The gap between design and purpose is central to the question of evolution and creation. Something may seem to be designed, but that does not necessarily prove that an intelligent agent made it with purpose. Crop circles, the Giant's Causeway, snowflakes and many other things seem so well arranged as to be artistic creations; but they are the results only of natural processes.

The nub of the issue is that evolution yields no scientific link to a creator or an intelligent agent. 'Intelligent design' scientists claim that science does point to such a link. Therefore, they demand that 'intelligent design' be taught in schools as scientific theory. Their opponents, however, think that that amounts to teaching religion – creation – pretending to be science.

American State schools are secular, and so they must exclude any religious teaching, Hence, the Courts decided that 'intelligent design' teaching must be excluded as well.

Assignments

1. View the film *Inherit the Wind*. Assess the balance in its treatment of the different characters and the two sides to the dispute. Where do you consider that the movie slanted its presentation of the story? What stance would you judge the film to espouse? In other words, on what side is the film director?
2. Write a note on creationism.
3. Compare and contrast the 'Big Bang' theory and 'creationism' as explanations for the origins of the universe.

By way of summing up the four cosmologies, two ancient and two modern, here is a diagram to encapsulate the main points about each. The four categories are presented in light of the following questions:

1. Whether the universe has a purpose beneficial to humanity or not?
2. Whether the evil in the universe came from the divinity-creator or from humanity or neither?
3. Whether the universe was designed intelligently by the divinity or not?
4. Whether the cosmology is open to the discoveries of science or not?

	BENEFICIAL PURPOSE	EVIL IN THE WORLD	DESIGNED BY GOD	OPEN TO SCIENCE
Ancient Babylonian	No	From the gods	No	No
Ancient Biblical	Yes	From humanity	Yes	Yes
Contemporary Big Bang	No	No	No	Yes
Contemporary Creationism	Yes	From humanity	Yes	No

Revision of Important Terms

Look up the following terms which you have come across in this chapter and briefly explain each one. Each of these terms is printed in bold in the text.

Cosmos, Cosmology, Galaxy, Nebulae, Light year, Doppler effect, Red shift, Entropy, Anthropic principle, Fine-tuning, Ancient cosmologies, Babylonian, Biblical, From Chaos through Conflict to Cosmos, From Void through Word to World, 'Big Bang' theory, Creationism, 'Steady State' theory, Continuous creation, 'Old Earth' creationism, 'New Earth' creationism, Intelligent design.

In summary...

Cosmology is the science of the universe. The universe is immensely huge and very ancient, at least thirteen billion years old. By comparison, humans seem very puny, but some cosmologists think that the human mind has a privileged place in the universe, and that humans were 'meant to be'.

The Babylonian Enuma Elish story depicts the beginning of the universe as a result of chaos, violence and conflict between the gods. The biblical Genesis story portrays the beginning as the product of intelligent design and careful order and loving purpose of the only God. These are two ancient cosmologies, though the biblical cosmology is the basis for the mainstream Christian cosmology today.

The 'Big Bang' cosmology, along with the theory of evolution, describes the beginning of the cosmos and emergence of life as the result of random chance and purposeless change. Creationists believe that the world was created by God exactly as described in Genesis, in seven days, with separate and stable species, with no need for billions of years of physical and chemical processes or the development of inorganic and organic life.

Chapter 9

The New Physics and Religion – Emerging Questions

(This chapter is for Higher Level students only.)

'Science without religion is lame, religion without science is blind.'

Albert Einstein

In this chapter you will learn about...

...how the new physics, the science of light, matter and energy, was revolutionised by Albert Einstein and his colleagues. Twentieth-century scientists proposed new answers to the eternal questions of light, matter and energy. A powerful technology showed that the new science is useful. Other questions arise as to how far it is true, and these affect philosophy and theology.

Resources for further study
See teacher's text on CD-Rom for further suggestions.

TIME AND RELATIVITY

ALBERT EINSTEIN (1879-1955)

This topic is also considered in **Section A, The Search for Meaning and Values**.

Coming up to the recent millennium celebration, *Time* magazine decided to run a feature on the 'Person of the Twentieth Century'. The magazine editors had an amazing variety of characters to choose from but, in the end, they picked Albert Einstein, because his ideas had an impact on so many aspects of life in the twentieth century.

Albert Einstein was born in Germany in 1879. His parents were Jewish, but the young Einstein received little religious education. Nevertheless, he was a questioning child. On graduation from secondary school, he failed to gain entry into the engineering faculty, but began studying physics and mathematics at university. He had to submit his doctoral thesis twice, before it was finally accepted.

Einstein could not get into a university as a lecturer and so he worked for the Swiss Patent Office. After work, he pursued his private research. In the year 1905, at the age of twenty-six, he wrote three articles that revolutionised science: on light as small particles, on the agitation of particles in liquid and, finally, on electromagnetism. These papers introduced a new approach to physics: the theory of relativity. This was Einstein's *annus mirabilis* (miraculous year).

Albert Einstein

Einstein was then offered a teaching job in Berlin, but by the 1930s the Nazi rise to power forced Einstein, with other Jewish physicists and mathematicians, to flee to the United States. Einstein became a professor at Princeton University. In 1939, he sent a letter to President Roosevelt in which he outlined the potential of uranium for use in weapons. The letter prompted the Government to develop the atomic bomb. Einstein himself took no part in the research, but instead involved himself in issues of world peace. He remained at Princeton until his death in 1955.

EVERYTHING IS RELATIVE

In the Newtonian world-view, space and time are independent of each other and of any other material thing or any movement. So far as the scientists of the last few centuries were concerned, space and time came before, contained and surrounded everything that exists and everything that happens. Space was the containing box, and time was the flow that carried events on its current.

Einstein was fascinated by puzzles about time. For example, if a light bulb suddenly flashed in a moving railway train, and it was seen by someone in the carriage, and by someone on the station platform, would the two observers see the flash at the same time?

Einstein solved all of these problems by a revolutionary solution: time and space are relative to the observer. The starlight that we see tonight is coming from events that happened millions of years ago. Are they happening now or did they happen then? Einstein's answer is that they happen *now* for us, but they also happened *now* for anyone who was near those stars at that time. There is no absolute time that applies everywhere. Hence his answer is called the **theory of relativity**.

There is, however, one universal, absolute, unchanging reality in Einstein's view of the universe. The speed of light is the same for all observers, no matter where they are or how they are moving. Light travels at 300,000 kilometres or a billion feet or 186,000 miles a second. This is the fastest possible speed. Nothing physical can travel faster. This is the universe speed limit for everything.

Time and Space

That insight changed the perception of time and space for scientists everywhere. Once again, the observer is back in the picture. It matters where the event was seen and who saw it. Observers would see things differently in different places at different times.

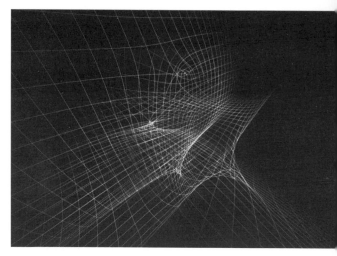

Instead of having four separate dimensions – three of space and one of time – we now have a **space–time continuum**. You can imagine this by thinking of your own movements from when you woke up this morning. You can map out your geographical locations: your bedroom, your diningroom, the streets you passed through, the school entrance, corridors and classrooms, until the spot you are in now. But you passed through all these places at particular times: 7.31 to the bathroom, 7.46 to the kitchen, 8.08 out the front door, and so on. Other people passed through these same locations, but perhaps at different times. You all traced different space–time lines through the space–time continuum.

Gravity, according to Einstein

The space–time continuum is not straight but curved. This is hard to imagine, as we can visualise only a three-dimensional space. One way is to picture a mattress with a heavy weight on it. It sags into the springs, and things placed on the bed will slip into the hollow. Equally, the space–time continuum curves around bulky objects, such as the sun or stars or planets. Things are drawn towards them and look as if they are pulled into them. This is Einstein's explanation for gravity. Newton had calculated its force, but Einstein's idea explained its action.

There are, however, very strange consequences for Einstein's insight. Time can go faster or slower depending on how fast the observer moves. Things may be bigger or smaller depending on how quickly they move. Suppose you are standing on a railway platform and you see a train passing by, going at over 100,000 miles per second! The train would look much shorter than its normal length and the clocks on the train would run slow. Everything about the train would be smaller or slower, *as seen from the platform*. But, *if you were on the train*, everything would be normal.

Questions

1. What do you understand by Einstein's theory of relativity?
2. What is a 'space–time continuum'?
3. What was Einstein's explanation for gravity?

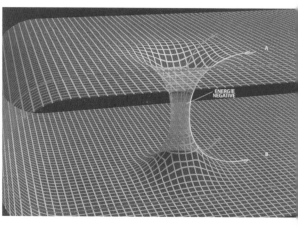

This cannot be tested on earth because the speed required is too high or the resulting difference too small. But at the great distances and huge velocities of outer space, or in the events of the subatomic world, though, Einstein's theory of relativity is necessary for measurement of what is happening. Only in the in-between realm of middle-earth, at our everyday speeds and human-size magnitudes, is Newton's science good enough for accurate calculation.

MATTER AND ENERGY

In addition to its effect on perceptions of time and space, Einstein's theory revolutionised ideas about matter and energy. He arrived at the (literally) explosive discovery: that matter and energy are so closely related as to be two forms of one reality. Matter is congealed energy, so to speak, while energy is dissipated matter. Just as ice, water and steam are different forms of the same chemical substance, but at different levels of potential energy, so all matter and all energy can be transformed from one to the other.

There is a huge amount of energy available in matter. Einstein's famous formula expresses that. $E=MC^2$. E stands for Energy, M stands for Mass (roughly speaking, equivalent to the Weight) and C is the speed of light. The formula says that the Energy contained in any given amount of material is the Mass multiplied by the Speed of Light multiplied by itself. That is a lot of energy.

When the Atomic Bomb Project created an explosion capable of devastating a city from a hunk of uranium that a child could carry in a school bag, Einstein's mysterious equation was illustrated tragically. Einstein's equation explains the explosion of the atomic bomb, the reason for radiation, the potential of nuclear energy and how stars burn.

Assignment
Assess the positive and negative implications of Einstein's famous formula $E=MC^2$. How did Einstein arrive at this breakthrough?

PARTICLES AND WAVES

LIGHT: WAVES OR PARTICLES?

Think of the 'Mexican Wave', when a football crowd starts jumping up and down in rhythm, but the motion sweeps through the stands around the stadium. Now think of a football, fired towards the goal, like a cannonball out of a gun. To which of these examples is light more similar? Is light like a wave spreading out from something in all directions? Or is light like a football shot in a straight line?

The question of whether light is a wave or is made up of particles, had been discussed since antiquity. Isaac Newton, for example, thought light to be particles, and, on that theory, he invented the science of optics. During the eighteenth and nineteenth centuries, the 'Wave' theory was dominant in scientific circles. A classic school experiment, the 'double slit', appeared to prove that light acted like a wave. A problem was that light had to *wave something*. Something had be shaking (oscillating) in order to be a wave. But light crossed empty space, filled with a vacuum. What could be waving in the vacuum? Scientists guessed that a medium called the *ether* filled the emptiness.

Mexican wave

In one of his 1905 articles, Albert Einstein proposed that light was indeed made up of particles. Light, he said, is comprised of **photons**. Instead of a medium waving, a particle or **quantum** (from the Latin meaning 'how much') is jumping from one location to another. In one move, Einstein had eliminated ether and also resolved many of the practical problems about light. His solution would be applied to matter itself by Nils Bohr, who suggested that everything was composed of particles, called atoms, with even smaller ones inside, called protons, neutrons and electrons.

Assignment

Assess the contribution of Nils Bohr in the struggle to understand quantum questions.

INSIDE THE ATOM

Nils Bohr

Nils Bohr (1885-1962), a Danish scientist, proposed a picture of the inside of the atom, similar to a little solar system, with a nucleus or core taking the place of the sun. The electrons revolved around the nucleus, like little planets. Of course, once we enter the subatomic world, we are describing realities that, by definition, are not the same as everyday material objects. Thus, to imagine the electrons and the nucleus to be little red and white billiard balls, as many of us do, is quite misleading. Little red and white billiard balls, however little they are, are made up of atoms and subatomic particles, which are quite different. Just how different they are, the next two decades would reveal.

QUANTUM QUESTIONS

Light (or radiation) then acts like a stream of particles. Electrons in atoms seem to act just the same as light. But the 'double slit' school science experiment shows that light can act as a wave. Can these modes of action be reconciled?

There are a number of possibilities. The first is that light acts in particle mode on some occasions, and in wave mode at others. The second is that light acts in particle mode and in wave mode at all times, hard as that is to imagine for us. The third is that we do not know, nor can we know, how light acts, but that it seems to act like particles, and also seems to act like waves.

Two scientists simultaneously developed calculations for dealing with light and, indeed, everything smaller than the atom. They did this work separately but in the same year, 1925. One was Werner Heisenberg; the other, Erwin Schrödinger.

WERNER HEISENBERG (1901-1976)

Werner Heisenberg was born in 1901 in Bavaria of a Lutheran father and a Catholic mother. At school he was always the head of the class, especially in mathematics and science. At university, he took up physics, achieving the doctorate in three years; not without trouble and pain, however, for he did rather badly in the oral examination, and the grades assigned by the board of examiners ranged from excellent to fail. In the end, he received a compromise pass.

In 1925, Heisenberg produced the first outline of what came to be called **quantum mechanics.** It has been described as a 'cookbook' approach; that is, a methodology to predict results without being able to explain what exactly is taking place. But this was the big breakthrough in the field, because scientists now possessed mathematics capable of measuring and predicting. The only problem was that the method could not be imagined easily. People could not picture the process lying behind the numbers.

There is an Irish footnote: the mathematics that Heisenberg needed for his calculations were invented by an Irishman, William Rowan Hamilton (1805-65), almost a century earlier. Hamilton discovered quaternion equations, the algebra for calculating in four dimensions. The idea struck him while strolling along Dublin's Royal Canal, and he carved the formula into the stone of one of the bridges lest he forget it. A plaque on Broome Bridge commemorates the event.

Resources for further study
See teacher's text on CD-Rom for further suggestions.

Werner Heisenberg

Questions

1. Explain Heisenberg's 'cookbook' approach.
2. Summarise his outline of 'quantum mechanics'.
3. What Irish footnote was there to Heisenberg's work?

> Here as he walked by
> on the 16th of October 1843
> Sir William Rowan Hamilton
> in a flash of genius discovered
> the fundamental formula for
> quaternion multiplication
> $i^2 = j^2 = k^2 = ijk = -1$
> & cut it on a stone of this bridge

Plaque on Broome Bridge

Erwin Schrödinger (1887-1961)

There is another small Irish contribution to the story. A blue circular plaque may be seen on the wall of a house on Kincora Road, Clontarf, in Dublin. 'Erected by the Irish-Austrian Society. Erwin Schrödinger. Born Vienna 12.8.1887. Nobel Laureate. Lived here from 1939 to 1956.'

In the 1930s, Erwin Schrödinger, like so many others, had been forced to flee Nazi Germany back to his native Austria, but Hitler's invasion there in 1938 drove him out again. He escaped to England, and was then invited by Eamon de Valera (himself a mathematician) to join the newly formed Irish Institute for Advanced Studies. So he arrived in wartime Dublin to settle down. He stayed until his retirement in 1956, when he returned to Vienna. He died at the age of seventy-four in 1961.

Erwin Schrödinger

Erwin Schrödinger's contribution to quantum mechanics was published in 1926. He dealt with light and electrons as if they were waves, and produced a suitable mathematical method called the 'wave equation'. Schrödinger was older than the other scientists working in the field, and his ideas were, accordingly, a bit 'old-fashioned'. He imagined the electrons and light as waves, and based his mathematics on that analogy. The result was a very practical method that scientists prefer to use.

The Uncertainty Principle

The obvious problem, both for the early quantum physicists, and for us, is that we cannot imagine what the subatomic world is really like. Hence, the use of picture words, such as orbit or particle or wave or whatever, cannot adequately describe what is going on. If we get the numbers right, however, we can say something useful.

Then there is an even more basic problem. To our shock, as we go further into the numbers, even they do not tell the whole story. This is the most famous feature of quantum mechanics: Heisenberg's **'uncertainty' principle**. It states that we cannot know the speed and the position of an electron at the same time.

There is a translation problem even in the title of the principle: 'uncertainty' is not quite the word that Heisenberg wrote in German. A translation closer to the original German would be **'indeterminacy'**.

Indeterminacy

In order to observe an electron, we have to see it. To see it, we have to bounce a particle of light off it. This impact, however,

Assignment

Explain Heisenberg's 'uncertainty' principle and its importance for science today.

126

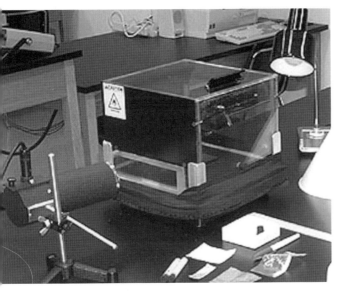

Cloud chamber

disturbs the electron in the act of observing it. Hence, it is impossible to determine both its speed and its location at the same time.

So, at first the Heisenberg principle looks like a defect in our way of knowing. The principle is saying that we cannot find out the speed and position of the electron because our instruments are not good enough. But, we may nurse the hope that a hitherto unknown technology, not involving particles of light, for example, may in the future find the answer for us. Hence, the principle is about 'uncertainty' on our part.

But the Heisenberg principle seems to cut deeper than that. For Heisenberg, the electron does not have a determinable speed and position at all in *itself*, whether or not we observe it. This is the direct conclusion from quantum mechanics. Subatomic particles are 'indeterminable'. Indeterminacy is not the result of limitations on human knowledge, but a fact of reality.

In other words, the electron is neither a wave nor a particle. It has neither speed nor position, until we 'determine' it by looking at it. When we have discovered either its speed or its position, the other information is no longer available. Our observation has apparently caused the electron to go one way or the other.

This fundamental property of matter and light and energy, as modern science reveals it, raises very interesting questions for the philosopher, the theologian and the ordinary person.

Assignment

'This fundamental property of matter and light and energy, as modern science reveals it, raises very interesting questions for the philosopher, the theologian and the ordinary person.' List some of these questions.

MATTER AND REALITY

'OH! REALLY?' MATTER AND REALITY

Bishop Berkeley of Dublin (after whom Berkeley Street in Dublin is named) taught the doctrine of **solipsism** ('one-self-ism'). Solipsism said that the only thing to exist is me. Every one and every thing else is a figment of our imagination, characters in our private video in the brain. Other things and other people do not exist.

How do we know that there is any thing real? How do we know there is something outside our minds? Maybe everything is a complex, three-dimensional, totally convincing dream?

This strange idea of Bishop Berkeley comes from the 1700s, after the time of Descartes. Solipsism assumes a huge split between mind and matter. This was, as we have seen already, a big issue for the Enlightenment. It runs through the history of nineteenth-century science, and accounts for much of the materialism and scepticism in contemporary culture.

But relativity and quantum mechanics have raised the same question in a more fundamental way. Does the world of quantum reality exist? Scientific instruments and mathematical procedures do not seem to put us in touch with anything that we could call real, factual, objective or true. Is anything actually there? If so, is it the result of a reasonable cause, or pure chance?

Assignment

Write a short essay tracing the origin and development of materialism and scepticism in contemporary culture.

THREE RESPONSES

We can give three answers to the question: Does anything exist? Do quantum realities really exist? We can say: Yes, No, or Maybe.

The 'Yes' or first position is **naïve realism**. This trusts our human sensation and perception as being completely and simply truthful, putting us into direct contact with the external world. For a naïve realist, there is no problem. 'What we see is what we get.'

For quantum reality, the realist believes that the instruments and measurements tell us that the particles and waves are really there. If their activities are puzzling to us at the moment, there may be more realities that we have not yet discovered.

But there are problems with naïve realism. We can be wrong. Things are often not what they seem. Our sensations and perceptions often play us false.

The 'No' or second position is called **instrumentalism**. It says that knowledge is useful rather than truthful. So long as what we know is useful, like a tool or instrument, then the reality does not matter. We are 'saving the appearances'.

Quantum mechanics helps us to predict subatomic events, but it does nothing to describe them or explain them. This is the Heisenberg position. We do not have to make sense of the results, just use them.

The 'Maybe' or third position is called **critical realism.** It maintains that we can discover the truth about reality, but admits that we can be very mistaken and plain wrong. Therefore, we need to check our conclusions. We have to be critical.

Scientists and theologians are normally critical realists. Therefore, we will be critical realists too, and we ask you, the reader, to take the same point of view – that is, if you really exist!

IS IT CAUSED? CAUSATION AND PROBABILITY

In the world of quantum physics, everything seems random. There is no strict link between an event and its consequence. We cannot determine the present due to the indeterminacy principle. What we can predict is only a probability that something may occur. To take an example, Iarnród Éireann might be able to predict with a fair degree of accuracy how many umbrellas will be lost each year on their trains, but they cannot predict, in particular, who will lose an umbrella.

Nils Bohr and Albert Einstein debated this point for decades. Einstein could not accept that the universe was random by nature; there had to be a mechanism that appeared to be chance, but was really completely caused. In a famous statement, Einstein said that God is not playing at dice.

Questions

1. Do you really exist? How do you know?
2. Which of the three positions makes sense to you? Explain your answer.
3. What does it mean to be a 'critical realist'?
4. What did Einstein mean when he said 'God is not playing at dice'?

A PLACE FOR GOD?

For the theologian, the randomness of quantum mechanics, like the natural selection of Darwin, poses a severe challenge. God, in the major Western world religions, causes things to happen. Can this be reconciled with quantum mechanics?

Some theologians perceive that the randomness of quantum reality is better for theology than the determinism of the Newtonian world-view. God was effectively isolated from the world by classical physics. In the new quantum universe, at least, there is plenty of room to admit God's intervention.

This topic is also considered in Section A, The Search for Meaning and Values; Section B, Christianity: Origins and Contemporary Expressions and Section C, World Religions.

God can, in the quantum universe, determine the potential position or speed of a particle, and resolve the indeterminacy. God can act in the quantum world by ensuring that quantum chance comes up right. God's action would not be scientifically detectable. All the cards would be on the table, the outcome would be perfectly open, it would seem to the spectators to be pure chance, but God could make sure that the quantum lottery is rigged.

ANOTHER GAP?

Other theologians caution against this opinion. They point out that past experience tells us not to get God to fill a gap where science lacks an explanation. The advance of science eventually squeezes God out of any gaps.

Another consideration is that there may be no gap to fill. Quantum science is a complete explanation. The clockwork science of Newton filled in all the connections to explain the movement of the heavens and the development of life in the universe. In the same way, the random process of quantum science is a full explanation of what happens. There is no need for God to get involved.

A third consideration is that it is hard to see how a divine intervention at the quantum level could have any effect on the macro level. Millions of subatomic chances would have to come up trumps for quantum events to exert a discernible effect on human life. God's intervention would be either completely negligible, or very obvious.

Fritjof Capra

FRITJOF CAPRA (1939-)

Fritjof Capra was educated as a physicist in Vienna and worked on particle research in Paris and California. Since 1972, he has been convinced that Western science has been moving closer and closer to the insights from Eastern religions.

In the preface of his classic *The Tao of Physics*, Capra relates the visionary moment that he experienced in the heat-haze on a beach as a young physicist. He tells us that he saw energy cascading from space, he sensed the elements, atoms and particles of his own body and the surrounding atmosphere and sunlight caught up in the creative dance that continually creates and destroys the material of the universe. 'I felt its rhythm and I heard its sound and at that moment I knew that this was the Dance of Shiva, the Lord of Dancers worshipped by the Hindus.'

Since this revelation, Capra has become an advocate for ecological education and a voice for holistic system thinking.

For discussion

1. Is there a place for God or a 'gap' for God in the quantum universe?
2. 'I felt its rhythm and I heard its sound and at that moment I knew that this was the Dance of Shiva, the Lord of Dancers worshipped by the Hindus.'
   What do you think Capra is trying to say in this statement?

Assignments

1. Outline two of the many ideas associated with the 'new physics'. Explain the importance of each of these for theological reflection.
2. Explain the 'holistic view' of the modern universe.

A HOLISTIC UNIVERSE

Quantum theory claims that matter can be both wave or particle; that is, spread out over space and confined to a specific position. A particle can be everywhere. A wave can collapse into a particular place. Space can be in motion. Everything is interconnected.

The lesson of modern physics is that the universe is one. Quantum experiments have shown that particles are part of a system, a complex, interrelated whole, holistic, interactive, organic and structured, rather than separated, individual, detached and isolated bits. Everything must be understood in the light of everything else. The whole is needed to explain any part. This is a **holistic view**. Accordingly, some thinkers, like Capra, have drawn the conclusion that there are similarities between Hindu and Buddhist thought and the findings of modern science, especially cosmology and quantum physics.

Theologians are doubtful about this because the analysis of concepts and ideas from another culture in an ancient language is a delicate and demanding task. One cannot do it by translations and the casual parallels of similar words, leaving aside the difficulty of ascertaining exactly what scientific terms and mathematical formulas really mean.

Dance of Shiva

One may conclude, though, that this is an area for research in the future, and it opens up room for collaboration between religion and science. As a symbol of this vision, and to commemorate the contribution of Indian scientists, the Indian Government presented the European Centre for Research in Particle Physics in Geneva with a statue of the Dance of Shiva. The plaque reads: 'It [the Dance of Shiva] is the clearest image of the activity of God which any art or religion can boast of.'

In summary...

Albert Einstein's theory of relativity proposes that matter and energy, time and space are all relative to each other. The observer's 'point of view' is reinstated in scientific discussion. Nuclear physics shows that matter is composed of particles, as is radiation, energy and light. Heisenberg and Schrödinger developed analytical procedures for studying the subatomic particles, called quantum mechanics.

Heisenberg's principle states that the speed and position of a subatomic particle could not both be determined at the same time. This is the 'uncertainty' or 'indeterminacy' principle. It raises issues of causality, of probability and of reality, which affect theology. Is there room for God's intervention at the quantum level? Or would that be another example of a gap soon to be closed by science?

Some scientists suggest that all of these considerations point to a more holistic and rounded view of the material and psychic universe.

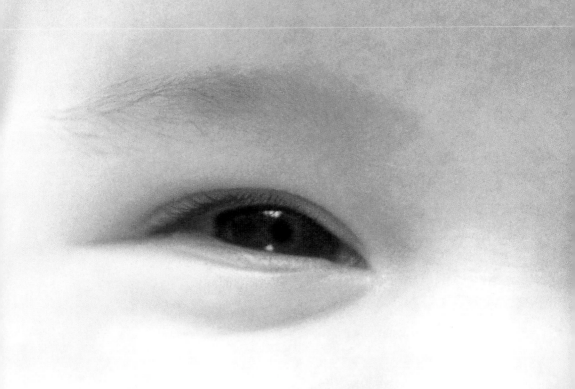

Part 4: Current Issues for Religion and Science – Life and Death

Note: In the fourth part, we turn to the questions posed by the new technologies of life and death. Students study *either* Part Three *or* Part Four.

Chapter 10

The Life Questions

'In the last analysis, it is our conception of death which decides our answers to all the questions that life puts to us.'

Dag Hammarskjöld

In this chapter you will learn about...

...the different views of the human being, provided by scientific reductionism and by religious belief. Issues include: What makes us human? What makes us persons? The chapter ends with an ethical discussion of the consequences of our view of the human being.

Resources for further study
See teacher's text on CD-Rom for further suggestions.

OPPOSING VIEWS OF THE HUMAN BEING

WHERE ARE YOU?

Close your eyes for a few minutes. Allow yourself to detach from your senses, your sight, your hearing, your smell, your touch and your taste. Direct your attention inward.

Now, where are you? Where do you imagine yourself to be? Where is the 'you' we were addressing? Where is the 'I' that responded?

This topic is also considered in Section B, Christianity: Origins and Contemporary Expressions; Section G, Worship, Prayer and Ritual and Section I, Religion: The Irish Experience.

Some people imagine the 'you' (or 'I') as in the head. They think of the *ego* (ego is the Latin for 'I') as a pilot, and the brain as a computer. Do you think of yourself in this way?

Other people imagine the *ego* to be in the chest or heart. For them, the self is a kind of engine or pump, the place of feeling and caring, of desire and drive. Do you think of yourself in this way?

More think of themselves as spread out throughout their

For discussion

How do you react when you are asked to focus on your spirituality? What connotations does that word have for you? Why is 'our spirituality of the body' one of the most important that we can have?

bodies, in even the big toe, or the little finger. Maybe that is the way you think of yourself. Is it?

Still others have no idea of themselves at all. They are just a temporary mood, or passing fancy, or fleeting thought, or momentary jab of pain or surge of pleasure. Do you think like that?

WHAT IS YOUR SPIRITUALITY?

This meditation is focusing on your **spirituality**; that is, your inward attitude or habitual way of thinking about something. How we usually think and feel and react to something often determines how we act towards it. Our attitude may not be well considered, or carefully decided, or even long thought about, but it could be crucial in how we behave and in what we do. It is important then to make sure that our spirituality, our inward attitude towards something, is what we want it to be.

Our spirituality of the body, that is, our inward attitude to our body, is one of the most important that we can have. It shapes our attitude to our whole self. It frames our view of the human being.

THE REDUCTIONIST VIEW

THE REDUCTIONIST VIEW OF THE HUMAN BEING

One common view of the human being today is that the human is nothing but the material elements that compose it. Many scientists hold that the individual human being is not a 'self' or an *ego* at all. Each of us is only the organisation of our physical and electronic ingredients. With death, the unity of these constituents is lost, and the 'self' dissolves.

These scientists say that the human being is nothing but a complex information-processing system, or a machine with a computer. They say that the heart is nothing but a pump for the blood, or the brain is nothing but a series of electrical exchanges and pulses, or love is nothing but a chemical reaction, and so on. In each case, the humanity is reduced to the material elements alone. This is **scientific materialism**.

Francis Crick

Francis Crick, one of the most famous scientists of the twentieth century in the area of genetics, talks about an 'astonishing hypothesis': '"You", your joys and your sorrows, your memories and your ambitions, your sense of personal identity and free will, are, in fact, no more than the behaviour of a vast assembly of nerve cells and their associated molecules...'

This is a reductionist view of the human being.

135

The clue to **reductionism** is the phrase 'nothing but'. The statement that something is nothing but something else is reductionist. It is so called because it reduces one thing to another.

Reductionism is a very common scientific approach to examining something. It means that lower things explain higher things. So, we can understand physical matter and energy if we know fundamental particles; we can explain biological life by knowing chemical interaction, etc. But it is one thing to use a method to reduce something to its basic essentials, and quite another to say that the elements are the only essentials.

Let us take an obvious example. A scientist describes falling in love in terms of hormones, genetic predispositions, chemical reactions and biological programming. But that description, alone, cannot do justice to the actual experience. There is a legitimate personal way for describing what happens to two people who are strongly attracted to each other, and we see it in novels, diaries, films, drama and poetry. This holistic view includes the personal. We recognise it as more rounded and experiential.

Reductionism is a useful scientific method, but it is not the entire measure of what we know. The heart is more than a blood pump; the brain is more than a computer; the human body is more than a machine; emotions are more than chemical reactions; ideas are more than electrical charges.

A reductionist is saying that the cake is only the recipe, the house is only the bricks, the symphony is only musical notes, and the novel only the alphabet in different combinations. A reductionist approach to science is like the fisherman who throws a net with a twenty-centimetre mesh into the water, and then declares, when he examines his catch, that there are no fish in the sea smaller than twenty centimetres. The scientific method has dictated the experience.

CONSCIOUSNESS

The reductionist view of the human person has still one huge unexplained area: consciousness. **Consciousness** means that a being knows something, and knows that it knows. Materialism as yet cannot explain how a being can be self-reflective. Our sense of identity, of being somebody particular, has, up to now, evaded scientific understanding.

Questions

1. What do you understand by scientific materialism?
2. How does this contribute to a reductionist view of the human being?
3. What is 'consciousness' and how does it help to negate reductionism?

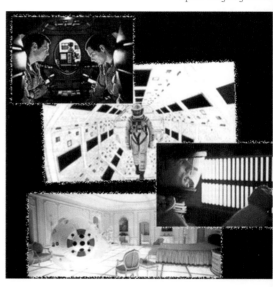

Space Odyssey 2001

Assignment

'What do you think? Will scientists ever explain our sense of identity? Our consciousness? If you say 'no', is not that just another 'God of the gaps'?'

Write a short note, attempting to answer the above questions.

Scientists are confident, however, that, sooner or later, they will be able to explain consciousness. They have been very successful with computer-generated artificial intelligence, in reproducing human ways of thinking. The supercomputer 'Hal' in Stanley Kubrick's film *Space Odyssey 2001* gives us a graphic imaginative picture of this.

What do you think? Will scientists ever explain our sense of identity? Our consciousness? If you say 'no', is not that just another 'God of the gaps'?

THE RELIGIOUS VIEW

THINGS WE DO

Think of all the things you do in the course of the day. You sleep, you wash, you eat, you drink, you walk, you talk, you work, you listen to music, you read books, you play football, you hum to yourself, you plan the weekend, you sit in class, you talk to a friend, you write a poem, you pray to God, you decide on a gift for your sister, and so on.

Make a list of your activities that involve only things that are present here and now.

Then make a list of your activities that involve things that are very far away or very far in the past, or very far in the future.

These two lists point towards another view of the human being. Some of the activities of the human being clearly are beyond or outside anything material, and they indicate another dimension to the human being.

Let us take an example. The pangs of hunger in your stomach may prompt you to plan dinner. We need go no further than that to explain your activity of planning to eat. Your dog or cat will do the same.

But what material element reminds you (a) that your brother likes pizza and (b) that it is his birthday and (c) that it would be good to have a meal with him? You are now dealing with things that are meaningful for spiritual reasons, and not for material ones. These suggest another dimension to human activity and to human beings.

THE RELIGIOUS VIEW OF THE HUMAN BEING

The human being is the only creature that God creates in and for itself. Therefore, the human being has special dignity, and ought not to be used or, indeed, abused for other purposes.

Human beings are rooted in the here and now. But human beings are also capable of abstract thought, creative imagination, eternal longing and enduring relationships.

Human beings exist in two realms: the material and the spiritual. This does not mean that human beings are divided things: a body separate from a soul; that is **dualism.**

The spiritual element is not totally explained by the material elements; that is materialism.

The same human being can exist in two distinct realms: the material and the spiritual. When you made the lists of the activities you engage in, the list of material things and the list of spiritual things, the one 'you' did them both. The same being, 'you', walked on the seashore and composed a poem about it.

The **religious view of the human** acknowledges that the individual human being exists in both spiritual and material dimension. The human being has an importance beyond the here and now, and possesses special dignity, moral significance and priority over the material.

Many religions believe that the human being will live for ever, enjoy immortality, or rise from death, because of the spiritual side of human nature. Christianity and Judaism say that human beings are created in the image and likeness of God, based on Genesis, Chapter one. Philosophy says that the human being is a 'person'.

WHAT IS SO DIFFERENT ABOUT HUMAN BEINGS?

On the last weekend of August 2005, eight people, five women and three men, spent three days in a cage in London Zoo

Questions

1. What is dualism?
2. What is materialism?
3. What is the religious view of the human being?

Resources for further study
See teacher's text on CD-Rom for further suggestions.

This topic is also considered in Section D, Moral Decision-making; Section F, Issues of Justice and Peace and Section G, Worship, Prayer and Ritual.

alongside the apes. The cage had the usual notice outside, except that it listed human beings as the exhibits, with their diet, habitat, world distribution, and threats to the species. A spokesperson for the zoo said that the idea was to show that human beings are animals, just like the apes.

Now here is a question: is there a difference between apes and us? If you say 'Yes', then what is the difference? What is it that makes human beings different?

For discussion

Make a list of possible reasons for the superiority of humans and discuss each of them.

Here are a few to get you going: strength, use of tools, ability for language, abstract thought, consciousness, originality, appreciation of beauty, morality and so on.

THE SIGNS OF DIFFERENCE

Let us go through the various candidates for difference, one by one. What is it that distinguishes the human being from the ape?

Is it strength? Many animals, including primates, are more powerful than a human being. So it cannot be strength.

Is it the use of tools? Some animals can use tools in a rudimentary way, though they do not have the ability to manipulate instruments as delicately as we can. They have little 'hand–eye coordination', as we say. But they can use tools. So the use of tools cannot be the difference.

Is it the use of language? Other animals are social and do communicate with one another. Jane Goodall discovered twenty-three different expressions used by chimpanzees, for anger, joy, surprise, etc. Are these language? Maybe they are. So it cannot be the use of language.

Jane Goodall

Is it being able to use abstract thought? Abstract thought is the employment of ideas independent of any immediate stimulation (*abstract* means 'drawn away from'). So when we think of parallelograms, or the galaxies, or honesty, or ancient times, then we are forming abstract concepts unrelated to concrete things that are immediately in front of us. These are abstract thoughts. Can animals think abstract thoughts?

We cannot get inside the head of an animal. We sometimes think that we 'can read the mind' of our pets by interpreting expressions or gestures – such as tail-wagging. Experiments have shown that it does seem that animals can use signs to convey their wants or other concerns. But this is quite different from using symbols and language in a context quite apart from an immediate situation, which would be required for abstract thought. So abstract thought, probably, is a distinctly human characteristic.

What about self-consciousness? Apparently, a chimpanzee can recognise itself in a mirror. That is basic self-consciousness. But human beings are aware of their own knowledge, of their own knowing, of their mortality, of their relationships, of their past and possible futures, and will make real changes in their lives as a result of this awareness. So awareness seems to be a particularly human phenomenon.

What about creativity and originality? Humans seem to be unique in their development of novel solutions to problems. By contrast, animals still use the same methods as they always have. An example is the bee, making combs to store honey in the same way for millions of years. So creativity is a special human quality.

Another area of human uniqueness is morality. Human beings are concerned about the 'ought' and 'ought not' area of living. This does not, of course, mean that they always, or even often, follow what they think they should. But they know what it is. Hence, moral responsibility is uniquely human.

By contrast, animals seem to be programmed to act in a fixed way. For moral knowledge and awareness, the actor needs to be really free. This seems not to be the case for animals, which act exactly as they were trained, or according to their instincts, or following their immediate wants and drives.

To sum up then, animals use tools, communicate, and may recognise themselves in a basic self-consciousness. But so far as we can see, and this has been investigated very extensively indeed, animals are incapable of abstract thought, creativity, original thinking and morality. These have to do with human awareness and human freedom.

Assignment

Summarise the signs of difference between animals and humans.

PERSONHOOD – WHAT MAKES US INDIVIDUALS?

WHAT MAKES US INDIVIDUALS?

An individual human is the same as an individual in all other species in this one respect: that the heap of matter, the particular material, the actual flesh of which they are made up is a different portion of matter, material or flesh.

The body of your dog is different from the body of your cat and different from the material that makes you up. The hunk of stuff is separate. It is as if the clay you took in your hand to form a clay dog is different from the next handful that you took to make a second animal.

This makes you individual and separate from any other human being. It makes dogs and cats and cabbages and trees and any being individually different from any other.

But that still does not pick out the individual human being as important or significant or unique...

Questions

1. If you were to meet a being from outer space, a true alien, a space-traveller, an extra-terrestrial (ET), how would you recognise such a being?

   What qualities would you look for?

   Remember that the extra-terrestrial may not look at all like us, or even like we imagine a being from another planet should look like.

   Suppose that such a being were a vapour, a wisp of smoke, or a light or glow?

2. Read Genesis, chapter two, where God brings all the animals to the first man, and the man names them, but finds no companion among them. Is not this situation exactly like the one we have just suggested?

   What is different about an individual human being when contrasted with the rest of the human race?

   Is there anything different about an individual human being, from, for example, an individual dog or cat, or chimpanzee or ape, or, for that matter, an individual tree or cabbage or an individual blade of grass?

   Take a moment to discuss that with your friends or to think it out for yourself.

The uniqueness, not just of the human race as a whole, but also of individual human beings, one by one, is something to do with their self-view, and their freedom to choose. The philosophers use two words to describe it: consciousness and autonomy. **Consciousness** is our ability to reflect on our own existence, to know something, and to know that we know it. **Autonomy** is our ability to make up our own minds for our own reasons.

The human being is a person. We look to other creatures that we may encounter, even those from outer space, for signs of consciousness and autonomy. These are clues of personhood. These seem to constitute the characteristics of a human being, the qualities of humanity, the uniqueness of humankind.

A **person** is a being with consciousness and autonomy. If I am a person, I know what is happening inside me, to me and around me, and I am able to decide what to think about it and what to do by myself.

We can put this idea another way: a person is capable of awareness and freedom. The phrase 'capable of' is important, as we shall see later. That phrase leaves personhood open for infants (not yet aware and free but will be so very soon) and the disabled, the sick or injured persons (who cannot be aware and free now, but were in the past, and may be again in the future.)

Human beings are the only beings so far discovered in the universe possessing consciousness and autonomy. We are the only beings who know what is going on in creation, who are able to explore it and who are able to develop a relationship with each other and with God who created us. This is the religious view of the human being.

The scientist cannot make statements like that. Scientists tell us that the human brain is the most complex and intricate organism discovered in the universe, and that its capability for processing of information is phenomenal. Further than that, they cannot go. It is not their fault. You cannot see God with a telescope. You cannot see human consciousness with X-ray.

HUMAN BEINGS AND GOD

Christian theologians and philosophers explored what it meant for human beings to be created 'in

Creation of Adam' by Michelangelo

Assignment

'What is a person?' Summarise what you have learned at this stage about the religious view of the human being.

This topic is also considered in **Section C, World Religions** and **Section D, Moral Decision-making**.

Resources for further study
See teacher's text on CD-Rom for further suggestions.

the image and likeness of God', and what it meant for Jesus Christ to be both 'true God and true man'. To answer these questions, they elaborated the concept of 'person'.

God possesses consciousness and autonomy. There are three Persons in one God. Out of God's consciousness and autonomy, God freely created the universe and all that is in it, including human beings.

We human beings are aware of our location in the world, our relationships to other beings in the world, our past, present and probable future, and acknowledge our free responsibility to the world, to other beings, to ourselves and to God.

BEGINNING AND END OF LIFE

SCIENTIFIC VIEW OF BIRTH

As we have seen in Chapter 6, Charles Darwin's contribution to the debate on the origin of humanity is this: he removed the element of purpose from the scientific explanation of life. In evolutionary theory, everything is understood as the result of natural selection and adaptation for survival. Even so astonishing an organ as the human eye can be satisfactorily explained by such a process extended over millions of years. Darwin's theory denied that a complicated living organism required an intelligent maker to explain its existence.

This is the **scientific view of the origin of life**. Living beings are material elements organised in a particularly complicated and interdependent way, capable of reproducing themselves. Life is a result of chance events and random variations in situations of difficult survival and scarce resources.

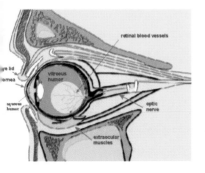

143

A lightning strike into the primordial ocean occasioned a chemical reaction. This caused single-celled organisms to appear, and the evolutionary process was underway. Or the first stirrings of life sprang into being on some other planet or asteroid, and arrived on our planet Earth with a meteorite. It is true to say that, scientifically, we are all made from star dust. But human beings, in themselves, according to the scientific view, have no more significance than being the result of a particularly fortunate series of accidents and happenstance.

RELIGIOUS VIEW OF BIRTH

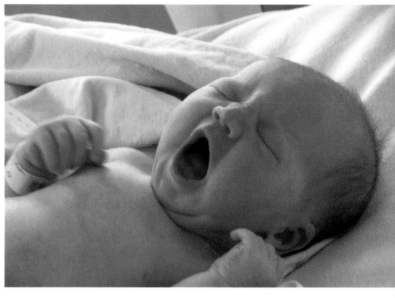

The **religious view of the origin of life** retains the concept of purpose and dignity. It regards the existence of human life as significant and meaningful, both for humanity and for the universe.

The religious view does not seek to explain the process of the development of life, but to recognise the dependence of life on God and to appreciate God's influence as the divine purpose that guides it to its goal. The religious person believes that God directs everything that happens, and that God has a purpose for every creature, especially each human being.

So the religious thinker cannot accept the complete absence of purpose, design and creation by a personal God. In so far as scientists insist that evolution means the denial of a Creator and a Creator's purpose for life, the religious person rejects evolution.

But some religious philosophers and scientists insist that science need not mean the elimination of God's creative action. In fact, they maintain, chance events and random variations make possible the free and open-ended course of life's history that we experience and that evolution requires. The closed, necessary and totally determined, mechanical, clock-like universe of Newton left no room for freedom, and hence no room for human autonomy or for God's creative and providential action. Contemporary scientific theories, including evolution, these thinkers suggest, leave ample room for both.

Assignment

Outline the 'scientific view of the origin of life' and the 'religious view of the origin of life'. Indicate areas where science and religion share the same concerns.

The **scientific view of the end of life** is materialist. As life is merely the interdependence and organisation of physical elements, so a breakdown in the coordination of these elements leads to dissolution of the material body and death of the human being.

The death of the organism is the end of the individual person.

The individual is never more than the random coordination of information and energy and will not survive the loss of coordination. The individual life will be extinguished, like a fire going out. Colour and movement and vigour depart and only the ashes remain.

RELIGIOUS VIEW OF DEATH

The **religious view of the end of life** insists on the importance of each human being and of every human life. This means that each person has eternal meaning and that human actions are of eternal significance. This view is true of every major religion in one way or another.

Samsara (The Circle of Life and Death)

Some religions, such as Christianity, Judaism and Islam, foresee that each member of the human race will survive beyond death. Death is a change of life, not its termination. Just as the *foetus* in the womb has no idea of what life outside its mother will be like, so the person in life can only speculate on the nature of life after death.

Other religions, such as Hinduism and Buddhism, do not believe in the immortality of the individual person. Nevertheless, they believe in the importance of human action and the outcome of free autonomous decisions. The consequences of a person's life-choices go beyond death. For Hindus and Buddhists, *karma* (the effect of human action) has an impact for the future, whatever it is.

FUNDAMENTAL ISSUES

'Is' and 'Ought'

If you own a washing machine, you will want to know how to work it. The rules for working a washing machine come from the mechanism itself. You look into it to see what it is and, therefore, how it ought to be used. The 'is' of the washing machine leads to the 'ought' of its use.

The same applies to human life. It matters what your vision of the human being is, because that will affect how you treat other human beings. If you think that certain people are a lesser kind of being, then that is how they will be for you. If you think, on the other hand, that people are important, then your actions towards them will be correspondingly careful.

This is why the scientific and religious views of human life are so important today. These views produce public policies and political decisions that will have consequences for our world in the future. We will look at some of these decisions in the next chapter.

Assignment

Outline the 'scientific view of the end of life' and the 'religious view of the end of life'. Indicate areas where religion and science share the same concerns.

Revision of Important Terms

Look up the following terms which you have come across in this chapter and briefly explain each one. Each of these terms is printed in bold in the text.

Spirituality, Scientific materialism, Reductionism, Consciousness, Religious view of the human being, Autonomy, Person, Scientific view of birth and death, Dualism, Religious view of birth and death.

In summary...

Our attitude to ourselves is the basis of our spirituality. Spirituality is the disposition whereby we approach our lives and our decisions. An important part of our spirituality is our view of the human being, our view of ourselves.

There are two opposing views of the human: the scientific, materialist view, that human beings are the physical elements only, and the religious view, that human beings consist of two dimensions, the spiritual and the material. These views result in different views of birth and death.

What makes us human? The difference between humanity and the animal kingdom could be physical strength, use of tools, ability for language, abstract thought, consciousness, originality, appreciation of beauty, morality and so on.

The human being, in the religious view, enjoys consciousness and autonomy, or awareness of self and freedom. Hence, the human being is concerned about morality, the 'ought' and 'should' of human life.

Chapter 11

The Genetics Debate

(This chapter is for Higher Level students only.)

'Life is nothing until it is lived; but it is yours to make sense of, and the value of it is nothing other than the sense you choose.'

Jean Paul Sartre

In this chapter you will learn about...

...the ethical or moral questions raised by the new scientific knowledge and techniques concerning human life. What if we can create life? Or at least produce it outside the bounds of nature? What if we can change the conditions of life radically? What if we can reproduce life to our own design? What ought we to do or not do? It begins with a general discussion of the reasons for morality.

Resources for further study
See teacher's text on CD-Rom for further suggestions.

This topic is also considered in Section A, The Search for Meaning and Values; Section B, Christianity: Origins and Contemporary Expressions and Section D, Moral Decision-making.

A TEST-TUBE BABY

Louise Joy Brown was born just after midnight on 25 July 1978 in the Oldham District General Hospital in Greater Manchester, England. She weighed five pounds twelve ounces. Her birth was big news all over the world, because she was the first baby to be born as a result of *in vitro fertilisation* (IVF). (The phrase *in vitro* means 'on glass', in contrast to *in utero*, which means 'in the womb'.) Louise Brown was the first 'test-tube baby'.

GENERAL PRINCIPLES

FIVE REASONS FOR MORALITY

What makes an action good or bad? Why would something be right or wrong? There are five answers, five moral reasons.

- The first answer is legality. The authority can be God, or the State, or the city or municipality, or the local district, or parents or teachers or whoever. We call this the Legal Reason.

- The second answer is the individual's authentic decision. It can be based on feeling or personal perception or sensitivity. We call this the Conscience Reason.

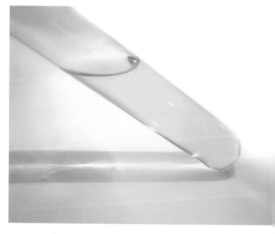

For discussion

Look at the five reasons for morality.
Assess each one in terms of its
applicability to your life and moral
decisions today.

● The third answer is the care of other human beings. The
  action itself is judged in so far as it is caring, whatever the
  situation. We call this the Loving Reason.

● The fourth answer is the result of the action in terms of
  happiness. This is the greatest good of the greatest
  number. We call this the Happiness Reason.

● The fifth answer is a religious or philosophical vision for
  the human person. We call this the Human Vision Reason.

DIFFICULTIES IN HAVING CHILDREN

Many couples discover that they cannot have children. There
may be a medical difficulty affecting either the man or the
woman. If there is a medical reason, even an emotional or
personal one, it is not necessarily anyone's fault. But people
persist in blaming themselves, at least in the back of their
minds, and this harms their relationship.

So there was hope when new medical techniques of human
reproduction opened up possibilities for childless couples.

A TEST-TUBE BABY

The doctors who assisted in the birth of Louise Joy Brown had
taken *ova* (eggs; singular is *ovum*) from the mother, fertilised
them with *semen* (seed) from the father on a dish in the
laboratory, and then put them back in the mother's womb to
be carried to a normal birth.

In vitro fertilisation (IVF) has since become a routine
procedure, with over a million births worldwide since 1978,
but it is successful in only about a quarter of cases. Many more
ova are fertilised than are needed for the IVF procedure, and
these are stored in refrigerators afterwards.

Questions

1. What is IVF?
2. What developments have taken
   place in this area since 1978?

Assignments

1. Assess IVF using each of the five
   reasons for morality. Which of
   these reasons would allow for IVF
   and which would forbid it?
2. The birth of Louise Brown brought
   to the world's attention the great
   promise and the great threat of
   medical advances. She was a 'test-
   tube baby' and the scientists had
   'played God'. What were the
   opportunities and threats of IVF as
   people saw them then? As you
   see them now?

For discussion

Media attention focused on the
normality of Louise Brown as a baby,
child, teenager and young adult.
Why do you think this was a theme
of the coverage?

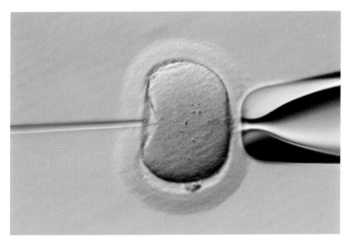

EMBRYOS

WHEN DOES HUMAN LIFE BEGIN?

There are different stages in the development of the embryo and each is claimed, by different scientists and philosophers, to mark the beginning of a new human being. These are: Fertilisation, Implantation, 'The Primitive Streak', Foetus, Brain Development, Viability, and Birth.

- *Fertilisation or Conception*: when the **semen** (seed) from the father combines with the **ovum** (egg) of the mother. Biologists agree that there is an unbroken and continuous process of development from that moment to birth.

- *Implantation*: when the fertilised ovum attaches itself to the walls of the uterus (womb). It is then called an **embryo** (from the Greek 'to be full to bursting within'). There are a number of fertilised ova in the mother, but only a few are fixed to the wall of the womb. **Implantation** happens a week after fertilisation.

- *'The Primitive Streak'*: when the embryo shows the beginning of a spine around the second week of pregnancy. Afterwards, the embryo will not split into twins. This is regarded as the definitive forming of an individual.

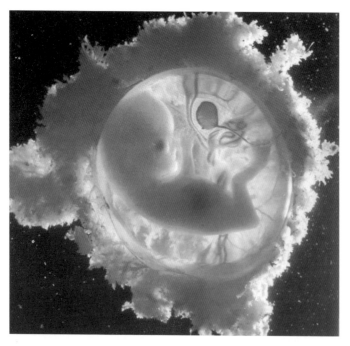

- *Foetus*: when the embryo assumes the distinctive shape of a human being. This happens about the seventh or eighth week of pregnancy. It is then called a **foetus** (from the Latin meaning 'offspring').

Questions/Assignments/ Group Work

1. Compose arguments based on each of these stages of development for the dividing line between the human being and pre-human material.
2. Some thinkers say that the relationship with the mother is the decisive element. The human being is by nature social. Therefore, the embryo has to become a child in order to be truly human. Which stage would support that argument?
3. Other thinkers argue that human functioning, thinking, being self-aware and so on, is the distinctively human quality. Which stage would support that argument?
4. Which stage would be most helpful to support an argument for someone justifying abortion, IVF, scientific research on embryos and so on?
5. Which stage, if agreed as the basis for public policy decisions and private conscience, would be most helpful for forbidding abortion, IVF, embryo research and so on?

For discussion

1. The rights of human beings should be respected, defended, cherished and nurtured. But parts of the body need not be accorded an equal standard of care. Should an embryo outside the womb be treated like a full human person? What should be its status in law? In ethics? In medical practice?

2. If an embryo is implanted inside the womb of a woman other than the biological mother, who has the moral or legal rights and responsibility for the child? The **surrogate mother** who bears the pregnancy? Or the biological mother who provides the egg? What are the rights and responsibilities of the father who provides the semen?

3. Some moralists and legal authorities emphasise the importance of gaining the consent of the biological mother before a fertilised embryo is used in any way. Is there a place for the consent of the biological father? What happens if they disagree? What is the status of the surrogate mother?

4. The Nazi government in Germany experimented with a programme of **eugenics** (Greek *eu* meaning 'good' and *gen* meaning 'birth'), to breed healthy and desirable people by eliminating unsuitable ones. This met with universal moral disgust. IVF provides the prospect of embryonic screening. Is this another form of eugenics?

5. The technique of IVF and cryostoring enables reproduction beyond the natural limits of human life, that is, after the age of pregnancy and after the death of the father. Some fathers have preserved semen for the fertilisation of their wives after their deaths. An Italian mother of sixty-two received a donated embryo and brought it to birth. Was it good for an elderly mother to have a child in that way?

● *Brain Development:* when the brain begins to function, which is around twenty weeks.

● *Viability:* A foetus becomes capable of surviving outside the womb around the seventh month of pregnancy, but with medical technology, the time will be pushed back further.

● *Birth:* The foetus emerges from the womb and becomes an infant. Civil law recognises a new human being, demands registration, and accords it the respect and rights due to a citizen.

CRYOSTORED PRE-EMBRYOS

Many doctors and scientists prefer the term **pre-embryo** for an embryo before implantation. The reason is that most legal systems do not recognise a non-implanted embryo as a person. The term 'pre-embryo' suggests that the unimplanted embryo is really sub-human. Many other thinkers use the one word 'embryo' because at all stages it is biologically a developing human being.

IVF procedures around the world have left hundreds of thousands of unused frozen embryos. These pre-embryos or embryos are kept in liquid nitrogen at a very cold temperature; that is, they are **cryostored** (Greek *cryo*, meaning 'cold and icy').

RELIGIOUS VIEWS ON NEW LIFE

Religious people have a special vision for the human being and approach these questions in a distinctive way. Christians believe that God creates each human soul and that each person is an image of God. They call the making of babies **procreation** (meaning participating in God's creation) rather than the scientific term **reproduction** (making a copy).

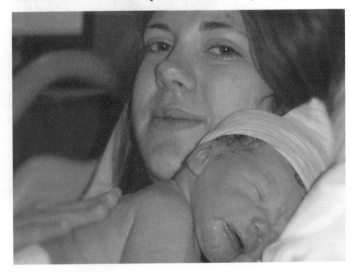

Many religious people, including Catholics, regard the embryo as a person, that is, an individual human being. Hence, they oppose the destruction of either embryo or foetus, because it is equivalent to killing or interfering with a person. This includes IVF and other procedures that place the embryo in jeopardy.

Marriage is, for Catholics, a sacrament, a sign of God's grace. Therefore, the act of intercourse between man and woman is intimate and should be reserved carefully for a married couple committed to each other. It is a natural process, but also sacred, and should not be interfered with artificially unless it is intended to correct a physical defect. This forbids donations of ova or semen, surrogate pregnancy, and various kinds of birth-control and contraception.

IVF may be done legally (in accord with a country's law), in conscience (parents and doctors act in good faith), with a loving intention (to give a child to a childless couple), and may come out well (a happy baby). These are the first four reasons for morality. Nevertheless, the Catholic Church and many other Christians do not consider IVF to be a loving participation in God's creation, and, therefore, it offends against the Human Vision Reason for morality.

GENES

GENETICALLY MODIFIED LIFE

James Watson

Two young scientists rocked the world in April 1953. Francis Crick (an Englishman) and James Watson (an American) published a 900-word article in the journal *Nature*. In this short piece, they proposed a structure for deoxyribonucleic acid (**DNA**) and noted that their proposed structure led immediately to a 'possible copying mechanism'.

Why the uproar? The reason was that they had discovered the chemical foundation for life. The 'copying mechanism' meant that it could reproduce itself, and that is one of the signs of living matter.

They found the now famous **'double helix'** structure for DNA: two linked strands, shaped like a spiral staircase, a twisted ladder or a long zipper. The rungs comprise the chromosomes and genes. These determine the characteristics of an individual. Half of an individual's genetic material comes from the mother and half from the father, and they combine in a new organism. When the double helix is 'unzipped', each side attracts a matching set of chemicals, and two zippers emerge where there had been one. This is the copying mechanism.

Francis Crick walked into the Eagle pub in Cambridge on 28 February 1953 with the announcement: 'We have found the secret of life.' He was a bit 'over the top' surely, but the discovery was truly momentous. It was one of the most important discoveries of the twentieth century.

THE SECRET OF LIFE

Crick and Watson's discovery of the 'double helix' encouraged researchers to press on with the task of understanding life in all its forms. **Genes** were described as 'building blocks of life', as 'blueprints', as the 'programme' or 'wiring' to explain growth and reproduction. Their images are suggestive: living things are built up with bricks, from plans, or programmes, or with wiring – engineering images.

The Double Helix

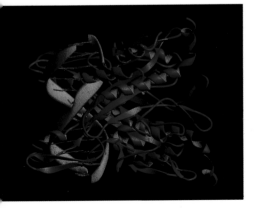

In the 1970s, scientists discovered how to change genes. They could 'insert', 'remove' and 'transfer' genes from one individual to another. This was called **'recombinant gene technology'**. Experiments proceeded with genetically altered plants and animals. Genetically altered crops were introduced, which could be resistant to different diseases or especially suited to different conditions. Many people have become very afraid of what has been happening, and want genetic alteration of plants and animals to stop.

ETHICAL CONCERNS ABOUT GENE TECHNOLOGY

Two fears seem to underlie the many objections to genetic alteration of animals and plants: safety and irreversibility.

Firstly, people are afraid that a laboratory may release a new strain of an organism that will be very dangerous. This fear of contamination should certainly make scientists and doctors very careful.

Secondly, people fear irreversibility. When a change is introduced into the DNA of an animal or plant, we have no idea where it will end. Once it is done, it cannot be undone.

Another concern is more emotional. People sometimes are afraid of any innovation. There is an argument for caution when dealing with innovation like this, but not necessarily outright condemnation.

A fourth anxiety is about the animals. Some people are concerned about exploitation of the animal kingdom. They say that animals have rights equal to human beings. They call the superiority of humanity over animals: **speciesism** (discrimination on the basis of species). They forbid any intervention in animal DNA.

For Christians, the human being is morally superior to the animal. Therefore, experimentation on animals is permitted if prudent, humane and necessary.

By contrast, intervention in human DNA should be a last resort. Manipulation of human genes should be forbidden if only because of the high risk of mistake. The rule for medicine is: 'In the first place, do no harm.' When risk is very serious and very probable, it does not matter how good the outcome might be. The chances for harm are too high.

HUMAN GENOME PROJECT

In the 1980s, scientists undertook the vast job of recording every human gene in DNA. This would enable joint research into genetic diseases and quick application of remedies if any were discovered. The **Human Genome Project** was launched formally in 1990 between the United States and partners in eighteen other countries. President Clinton and Prime Minister Blair announced the completion of the first survey of the human genome on 26 June 2000.

The **genome** is the entire DNA sequence of a living organism. Genes command the manufacture of the proteins that regulate how the organism looks, how it works and how it behaves. There are three billion bases in the human genome, and if they

Resources for further study
See teacher's text on CD-Rom for further suggestions.

Question

Explain clearly the following terms: DNA, Genes, 'Recombinant Gene Technology', Speciesism.

For discussion

1. Have you fears about the genetic alteration of plants and animals? What are they? Would you trust scientists and laboratories to do it safely?
2. What are the problems with genetic alteration that do not apply, for example, to selective breeding?
3. What about the genetic alteration of animals as distinct from the genetic alteration of plants and crops?
4. What about the genetic alteration of human beings?

Tony Blair

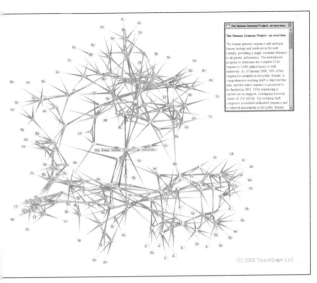

(C) 2002 TouchGraph LLC

The human genome

were written in a book, they would fill two hundred telephone directories of a thousand pages each.

The human genome is the actual blueprint for human beings – as promised by Crick and Watson in 1953. We can expect new ways to prevent, treat and cure illnesses, particularly hereditary diseases such as Huntington's chorea and cystic fibrosis, to emerge from genome research. With genetic information, patients may be warned if they are at risk of certain diseases, decades before the symptoms will show.

ETHICAL CONSIDERATIONS ABOUT GENETIC INFORMATION

The problems that arise in relation to genetic information are similar to those that confront professionals in other situations. Is one obliged to give all the information about an illness that may occur in years to come? The duty 'not to harm' may conflict with the duty to 'tell the truth'. The doctor may fudge the answer, not tell the whole truth, to give hope to the patient.

There is an argument that no more information or knowledge should be sought than can be acted upon for the good of the individual concerned. In other words, medical personnel and civil authorities should not try to find out things that will not help the person, cannot lead to treatment, and may be positively harmful to the person, if widely known. Thus, from the point of view of the patient, genetic information may be the type of information that, for the moment, it is better not to know.

For discussion

1. The ownership of genetic information is the ethical issue. What if private companies patent particular genes or gene therapies that they have isolated, and charge for usage?

2. Another question arises if prediction of future disease becomes possible. Should medical authorities inform individuals, or their parents, if they are likely to develop a disease in the future? What are the ethical limits on information-gathering and dissemination, when it concerns the medical history or destiny of individuals?

3. Should civil authorities forbid marriage, for instance, or set limits in any way, for citizens identified as a health risk in the future? Should we block particular careers for people prone to certain diseases?

4. Suppose, for example, a gene for violence were discovered in an infant. One can imagine a situation in which the State would want to 'treat' such a young person if it was known early enough. Would it be legitimate or ethical or caring or useful or humane to tell the public authorities?

CLONES

A little lamb was born in Scotland late in February 1997. 'Dolly' was the first identical copy of a single animal. It was a **clone**, the offspring of one parent without the assistance of the other parent. Dolly's birth meant that the same could be done with human beings.

Ian Wilmut and Dolly

The Roslin Institute in Edinburgh, led by Ian Wilmut, had accomplished the feat. The technique was to take the nucleus of an adult sheep's body cell and place it into an egg from which the nucleus had been removed. So instead of the mother's genetic contribution in the ovum, both male and female genes were present in this cell, copied from another adult sheep. It was 'zapped' with electricity to activate it, and placed in a surrogate mother sheep and the pregnancy brought to term. The result was a lamb that was an exact copy of the adult sheep that provided the nucleus. This technique is called **somatic cell nuclear transfer** (*soma* is from the Greek, meaning 'body'.)

The news of Dolly was disturbing because the technology was now in existence and readily available in medical laboratories. People anticipated that an attempt at human cloning was not far in the future. Human cloning is illegal in the United Kingdom, and a moratorium (legally authorised delay) on human embryo manipulation was asked for in the United States, but it was clear that unscrupulous doctors would try the procedure in another country that would not be careful about the moral implications.

Intervening in human embryonic development is a serious moral problem. Opinions differ according to views on the status of the embryo. According to the moral stance of different faiths, the embryo may enjoy the moral rights of an adult human being (for Catholics), or simply deserve special moral respect (for many other beliefs), or be no more special than any other part of the body. But the cloning of human beings seems, at present at least, to be abhorrent to a wide spectrum of public opinion.

Let us examine human cloning from the perspectives of each of the five reasons for morality.

The Legal Reason depends on the legislation in the country as to whether or not it is allowed. Most countries forbid it at the present time. But that could change, and probably will change.

The Conscience Reason would rely on the feeling or immediate perception or emotional reaction or moral conviction of the persons concerned. Most people at present regard cloning with loathing; that is, they object because of the 'yuck' factor.

The Loving Reason takes into account the concern and attention that may be shown in a particular attempt to clone. The sympathy towards women who, for whatever reason, cannot have a child with sexual intercourse, could come into play here. On the other hand, one might question the wisdom of the intention to replace a young child tragically killed in order to console the grieving family.

The Happiness Reason assesses the final outcome or consequences of introducing this procedure. This could include the mistakes and the surplus embryos, as well as fears that dictators will clone less intelligent human beings to exploit them, or more intelligent human beings to help them dominate.

The Human Vision Reason addresses whether cloning is appropriate for the human vision of a person. Religious authorities have generally held that cloning is a mechanical production of new life, and is contrary to the vision of what a person is.

DESIGNER BABIES

Molly Nash of Englewood, Colorado was born with Fanconi's anaemia, an inherited disease of the bone marrow. She would eventually die by the age of seven after a distressing illness. The only known cure is to transplant healthy cells from the umbilical cord blood of a brother or sister who is a perfectly matched donor. No such donors were available for Molly.

Molly's father and mother, Lisa and Jack Nash, had a 25 per cent chance of conceiving a child with the same inherited disease. They could try the IVF procedure, with a screening to make sure that the resulting baby would not be subject to the disease. They tried it four times, but none of the attempts ended in pregnancy. Then on 24 December 1999, they learned that Lisa was pregnant. Adam Nash was born on 29 August 2000, and the transplant was performed in October. Molly was then six years old, and she held Adam in her lap during the procedure. Since then, Molly and Adam have been well and healthy.

This was, of course, not an example of cloning, but it shows a reason why cloning could happen. Adam Nash was conceived 'to order' to provide a treatment for the illness of his sister,

For discussion
1. Discuss the prospect of the cloning of human beings.
2. What do you anticipate happening in the future?
3. Suppose it became inexpensive enough for wide application, why would people seek its aid?

Molly. It is true that she would not have lived without the transplant. It is also true that he would not have existed at all without her illness and need. Ten other embryos were discarded and destroyed in the search for the right one. Adam Nash, then, was the first 'designer baby'.

Adam Nash was the result of a straightforward IVF procedure, making use of the genetic material from both father and mother. **Reproductive cloning** is an IVF procedure using the genetic material from one parent only. Reproductive cloning creates an exact duplicate of the individual providing the nucleus of the cell, and the two will be genetically identical. They will be similar to identical twins, except that the donor will be older than the clone.

THERAPEUTIC CLONING

Christopher Reeve was a celebrity when he was selected to play Superman in the movie of 1978. But he became a real-life hero when, in 1995, he suffered a horrific accident in a fall from a horse, which left him completely paralysed. After a challenging recuperation, he turned into an energetic activist for the disabled and the most famous promoter of stem cell research. This was because he believed that it would soon be possible to repair his spinal cord, and heal similar disabilities, with **stem cell replacement therapy**. Unfortunately, Christopher Reeve died on 11 October 2004, at the age of fifty-two, before his dream could be a reality.

The reason why stem cell replacement therapy might work lies in the nature of the stem cell. Most cells in the human body are **differentiated somatic cells**; that is, they can only grow into one portion of the body, whether limb or bone or nerve or skin or organ. Stem cells, by contrast, are **undifferentiated somatic cells**, and have the ability to become any one of a range of different cells.

It is easy to see that stem cells are very valuable 'Mister Fixits'. Inject some into the spinal cord or another part of the body, and, given time, they will strengthen a weakness or seal a gap. Already, medical researchers are working on different applications with some successes.

Therapeutic cloning is done by developing a cloned embryo to the stage where it is possible to obtain an organ, skin, nerve or enough stem cells from it to help treat another individual. At the present time, many scientists regard the embryo, produced either by somatic cell nuclear transfer (the 'Dolly' technique) or by fertilisation of an ovum (IVF), as the preferred source for stem cells. This is the reason for the vigorous moral objection to the technique being applied to humans. A human embryo is destroyed in the process.

For discussion

1. Saving Molly's life was surely a worthy cause. But there are other possible causes. What would you think about designing babies with enhanced intelligence, good looks, athleticism or some other quality? How would you distinguish between a worthy and unworthy cause?
2. One clinic in the USA is offering to help parents select the gender of their child by employing genetic screening. What do you think about that?

Question

What do you understand by cloning, therapeutic cloning and stem cell research?

Christopher Reeve and family

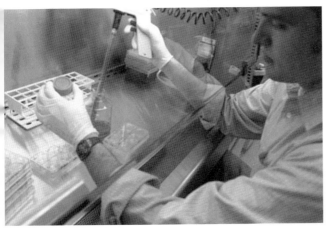

The Stem Cell Debate

Where else, then, could we procure stem cells? There are at present three main sources: we can get them from early embryos, or directly from adult stem cells (the patient's own adult stem cells), or from umbilical cord blood and the birth placenta of a newly born baby. The debate centres on the use of early embryos. These embryos exist in great quantities, preserved frozen in fertility clinics around the world, left over as extras from IVF procedure.

Question

What are the moral issues that the use of early embryos raises for stem cell research and therapeutic cloning?

This topic is also considered in **Section D, Moral Decision-making**.

Views on Stem Cells

To those who regard the embryo as a true human being, using it as a stem cell supply is the moral equivalent of abortion. This is the moral position of many religious and ethical groups, including the Catholic Church.

Others oppose stem cell research with embryos because they do not trust drug companies. Stem cells can be used for testing new products on humans, for example. Objectors suspect that drug companies are using the case of the spine-injured patient to gather support for research that would have a commercial purpose.

Still others object to the emphasis placed by this debate on the disability of spinal injury, as though these patients are particularly disadvantaged in their quality of life. They point out that many of them enjoy personal relationships, social acceptance, happiness and fulfilment that is at least as good as the average person.

Reprogramming Cells

As mentioned above, there are other sources for stem cells: adult somatic (body) cells and the cells of the umbilical cord. The placenta and umbilical cord are normally discarded after birth. Stem cells derived from an individual's own umbilical cord would be more useful than donor stem cells. So we are beginning to see umbilical cord blood preserved in order to provide an individual source of stem cells if needed. There is no debate about this procedure, as all sides find it morally unobjectionable.

Equally, somatic nuclear transfer techniques may soon produce stem cells capable of replenishing bodily tissue and organs. A procedure that avoids the 'cloning' stage would not be objectionable on the grounds of killing an embryo.

Finally, there would be no moral objection, were it possible to reprogramme body cells into stem cells. Scientists are very hopeful of an early breakthrough in **somatic cell reprogramming** – also called **'dedifferentiation'**. This would be a procedure with which all could morally agree.

Assignment
Explain clearly why 'dedifferentiation' is a procedure with which all could morally agree.

DEATH AND DYING

PROLONGING OR ENDING LIFE

In the spring of 2005, two people entered a long decline into death. One was a woman in the United States, the other was a man in Italy. They were both to die with the attention of the world upon them.

Terri Schiavo

The American woman was Terri Schiavo of Florida. She suffered severe brain damage in 1990 after a heart attack and was left in **'a persistent vegetative state' (PVS)**. This means that the person is alive, wakeful, with involuntary and reactive movement, but with no apparent human consciousness and no hope of improvement. She could not communicate and appeared to be completely unaware of those around her. She had to be fed and given water artificially with a feeding tube through her stomach wall.

Terri's husband, Michael Schiavo, and her parents, Mr and Mrs Robert Schindler, disagreed about what to do. Her parents wished her to be cared for until she died. Her husband wanted to end the care, remove the feeding tube, and let Terri die. The debate eventually involved the Catholic Church, for Terri was a Catholic. After a long court case, the feeding tube was removed on 18 March, and she died on 31 March 2005.

The man in Italy was Pope John Paul II. He had been nearly killed in 1982. By 2000, he was suffering from Parkinson's disease and other ailments. In early 2005, he went into a decline. In the glare of the world's media, he tried to fulfil his normal duties during Lent, then succumbed to his illness, and died in the first week of April, a few days after Terri Schiavo.

Many commentators linked the two deaths, for the contrast could not be clearer. In the case of Terri Schiavo, human life was judged as worthy of preserving in so far as it was productive, conscious and happy. In the case of the Pope, a human life was seen to be valuable on its own terms, whether

Pope John Paul II

Assignments

1. Leaving aside complications in the Schiavo case (such as the motives of the husband and of the parents, and the political aspects), what are the issues in the care of PVS patients?
2. Outline the three rules that apply to the ending and prolonging of life in Christian moral thinking.

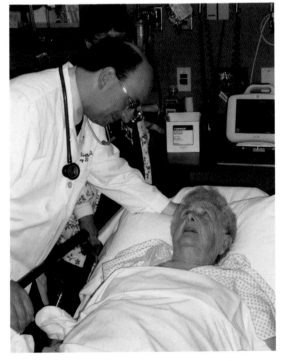

the person was healthy or sick, happy or sad. In fact, Pope John Paul II showed suffering to be even more effective, silence more persuasive, and weakness stronger than health, speech and strength.

THE OBLIGATION TO PROLONG LIFE

Many of the issues attending the ending and prolonging of life arise in the Schiavo case. There are three moral rules applied to these situations in Christian moral thinking.

The first rule is that treatment should prolong life, not the process of dying. This means that the doctor or medical personnel or family has to decide: is the proposed treatment likely to benefit the patient without undue hardship? Or are we just extending the length of the person's dying?

The second rule is that we are morally obliged to use the ordinary means (methods) of preserving life. **Ordinary means** are ones that are normal and routine, part of a regular duty of care, and should never be denied to oneself or another. **Extraordinary means** are out of the ordinary, either because of expense, or rarity, or suffering, or inconvenience, or the small hope of recovery. Extraordinary means of treatment are optional.

An example will make this clearer. Suppose that a person is suffering from a rare disease. When he first experiences the symptoms, he is obliged to take ordinary care of himself. This certainly includes going to the doctor for an examination. It will also ordinarily include attending a specialist, if referred by the doctor. Nowadays, in developed countries, medical care and hospital care constitute an ordinary means of preserving life and health.

If, however, this disease is so severe or so rare that the regular treatments do not work, another situation arises. The patient is not obliged to go further. She may refuse drastic surgery, high-risk therapy, expensive procedures, courses of treatment that would require a long time, a far journey, great pain. She may also have these treatments as well if she wants them. They are optional.

The third rule is one that applies to many medical and moral problems. It is described as the necessity for **'informed consent'**. This means that the patient must freely agree with any course of treatment, and have enough information and knowledge to know what is being done. This does not mean that the patient needs to have the knowledge appropriate to a doctor. It is sufficient that the patient is aware of the likely outcomes, the possibilities and the side-effects of what is proposed. If the patient is not capable of informed consent, then the next-of-kin must discharge this duty in the interests of the patient.

APPLICATION TO ACTUAL CASES

In the case of Terri Schiavo, a number of questions come up, each related to one of the medical rules.

The first question relates to the rule about extending the process of dying. Terri Schiavo was physically very healthy. Her bodily reactions and functions were working well. She needed no assistance to breathe, and her heart worked perfectly. She lacked awareness and conscious action and, for this reason, she needed help to eat and drink. Therefore, it seems as if Terri Schiavo was not dying at all. A patient who needs a respirator to breathe, and who will die promptly when the respirator is turned off, is clearly in a different situation to Terri Schiavo.

The second question relates to extraordinary means. This concerns the feeding tube. Terri Schiavo had to be fed by a tube into the stomach. If a feeding tube is normal care, it is an ordinary means of preserving life. If a feeding tube is not normal care, then it is an extraordinary means of preserving life. The problem is that methods that were once extraordinary, can, with progress, become ordinary.

What, then, is a feeding tube? It does require skilled attention, but nowadays it is pretty routine and not very expensive. The withdrawal of the feeding tube looks as if the doctors did not just let her die, but denied her an ordinary means of preserving life. A feeding tube might be legitimately removed if the patient could no longer eat or digest food or if its reinsertion would cause distress. This was the opinion expressed by Pope John Paul II himself in 2004.

Assignment

There have been three well-known cases similar to the Terri Schiavo case. Research one of them and compare it with this one. Which moral conclusions would you come to? These cases are: the Karen Quinlan Case (New Jersey), the Tony Bland Case (United Kingdom) and the Ward of Court Case (Ireland).

A final question relates to informed consent. Terri Schiavo's husband, Michael, claimed that Terri did not want to survive on a machine, and the court accepted his evidence. Others judged that Michael was arguing for his own interests, rather than the best interests of his wife. The next of kin giving informed consent for the patient does so as a good-faith trustee. The trustee must have the patient's good at heart. This was called in doubt by the Schiavo case.

Resources for further study
See teacher's text on CD-Rom for further suggestions.

SELF-DETERMINATION IN DEATH AND DYING

Dr Jack Kevorkian is a prisoner in the Thumb Correctional

Dr Jack Kevorkian

Assignments

1. Few countries or states allow for assisted suicide or euthanasia. If you were a legislator considering such a law, which safeguards would you think necessary? For example, who should propose or decide on euthanasia or assisted suicide? Who should be allowed to assist? Should there be any necessary or legal conditions, or should the procedure be entirely a matter for individual decision?

2. Construct arguments for assisted suicide or voluntary euthanasia. On what moral principles (of the five suggested previously) are these arguments based?

Facility in Lapeer, Michigan He is serving a sentence of ten to twenty-five years for murder, for the 1998 *euthanasia* of Thomas Youk, who suffered from a form of motor neuron disease. Kevorkian, seventy-five years old, is due for release in 2019.

Dr Kevorkian became known world-wide in the 1990s as 'Doctor Death'. For twenty years, he conducted a campaign for the right of patients to determine their own time of death. He promoted the 'right to die' for patients who were suffering excessive pain or experiencing severe disability. He professed himself ready to help with **doctor-assisted suicide**, making it easy for patients who might otherwise be unable to cause their own death.

Doctor-assisted suicide means that the doctor enables patients to kill themselves. Euthanasia is different. **Euthanasia,** also called mercy-killing (from the Greek *eu thanatos*, 'good death'), means that the doctor, or another person, actively and directly causes the death of the patient.

Kevorkian constructed an automatic machine to administer lethal drugs to a patient intravenously. He would attach the machine to the patient's arm, and leave to the patient the simple act of throwing the switch. He began offering the service of assisted suicide in 1991, carrying out the procedure in a caravan in a car park, or in a hotel room, or in the patient's own home. By the late 1990s, he had assisted, on his own claim, in over one hundred such deaths.

In 1999, in order to enlist the support of public opinion, he allowed CBS to record the death of Thomas Youk. When CBS broadcast the tape on *Sixty Minutes*, the law had the evidence to jail him.

QUALITY OF LIFE

Doctors frequently speak of a patient's **'quality of life'**. By this they mean the ability of the patient to interact with family and friends, the awareness with which the patient may live life in the future, and so on. A bedridden, painful and sedated existence is not rated as enjoying a high 'quality of life'. This rule is used to make decisions about operations to save life and procedures to prolong it. It can be applied at the beginning and at the end of life, to decide on the life chances of a foetus in the womb or of an elderly person on life-support.

The problem with the 'quality of life' discussion is that it emphasises the visible aspects of living and overlooks the spiritual side entirely. The value of suffering and sacrifice is ignored. The difficulties and burdens of family and community are over-emphasised and confused with the condition of the patient.

It is better to confine discussion to whether the benefit *to the patient* is worth the cost (including human costs, such as pain) of the proposed treatment. An assessment of the proportionality of benefit to cost avoids abstract judgement on the value of life and directs attention to the medical issues on which doctors are qualified to pronounce.

HUMAN AUTONOMY

The freedom of the individual human person is a fundamental issue in moral thinking, Christian or contemporary. This is called autonomy and it is one of the values that Christianity and Western civilisation share. The participation and consent of the patient and the patient's family is morally required.

Assignment

Outline the ethical issues that arise in science and religion in relation to *two* of the following:
- artificially created life;
- genetically modified life;
- cloning;
- the prolonging of life;
- the ending of life.

Another fundamental in moral thought is the distinction between things that happen and things that are made to happen. People die every day. That does not justify anyone actively and directly causing people to die. It may seem to be good that someone should die quickly, but that is no argument to prove that anyone should kill him, or that he should kill himself. This is the objection to euthanasia. Euthanasia provides a licence to kill.

Christians have a deeper objection to euthanasia. The Christian view is that life is a gift from God. We should not willingly reject the gift of life that God has given us. We do not

own our lives; rather, we are stewards of our lives. Every human being is a creature of God, made in God's image. This means that every human life is precious.

For the Christian, death has meaning and power. A person's life parallels the life of Jesus, the Son of God made man. The death of the Christian partakes in the death of Jesus on the cross. Accordingly, the Christian can freely face death, make decisions about dying, put up with pain, courageously try to continue living as long as God allows, and graciously accept death when it comes. This is what John Paul II's death demonstrated to the watching world.

Revision of Important Terms

Look up the following terms which you have come across in this chapter and briefly explain each one. Each of these terms is printed in bold in the text.

In vitro fertilisation (IVF), Semen, Ovum, Embryo, Implantation, Foetus, Surrogate mother, Eugenics, Pre-embryo, Cryostored, Procreation, Reproduction, DNA, Double Helix, Genes, Recombinant gene technology, Speciesism, Human Genome Project, Genome, Clone, Somatic cell nuclear transfer, Reproductive cloning, Stem cell replacement therapy, Differentiated somatic cells, Undifferentiated somatic cells, Therapeutic cloning, Somatic cell reprogramming, Dedifferentiation, Persistent vegetative state (PVS), Ordinary means, Extraordinary means, Informed consent, Doctor-assisted suicide, Euthanasia, Quality of life.

In summary...

In this chapter, we learned about different moral perspectives as they are applied to the new technologies of birth and death. Catholics and others morally object to IVF because it mechanises procreation and offends against the dignity of the human being.

Stem cell research and techniques currently involve the destruction of embryos, which many Christians and other moralists believe to be potential or actual human beings. Stem cell research and therapy that does not destroy embryos is morally acceptable. Gene experimentation with plants and animals should be carefully conducted to avoid disastrous results. Human gene experimentation should be even more careful not to harm anyone.

Moral or ethical considerations concerning the end of life involve the medical distinctions between prolonging life or the process of dying, ordinary and extraordinary means, direct killing or permitting natural death, and the requirement for informed consent.

Chapter 12

Conclusions

'I see it well: my mind will never be at peace,
till that Truth dawn upon it which hides
no further truth beyond itself...
it is our nature that such questions spur us
from hill to hill onward towards the summit.'

Dante, Paradiso, IV, 124-132

In this chapter you will learn...

...to consider some general approaches to the relationship between science and religion. First of all, we examine the argument that Christianity, far from being a block, actually helped the rise of science in European culture. Then we look at three options for the science and religion relationship: that they are in conflict; that they are independent; that they should be collaborative. Finally, we suggest a general framework that may provide a perspective from which God's presence to the universe may be considered.

CHRISTIANITY AND THE RISE OF SCIENCE

Modern science developed in Western Europe during the Middle Ages in a society dominated by Christian beliefs and social structures. Why did science arise and thrive first in Christian Europe, and not in the other great civilisations, like India, Egypt, China or even ancient Greece?

Hereford Cathedral

The medieval approach was based on the thinking that science and religion were in complete harmony. For most of their history, modern science and Christianity were regarded as going hand in hand. The first scientists were Christians who saw it as their religious duty to explore the world in order to give praise to its Creator.

Christianity had some basic convictions that helped people unlock the secrets of nature and develop new knowledge about the material world. Some historians of science have proposed that the Christian doctrine of creation in particular encouraged the rise of science in the sixteenth century.

THE UNIVERSE IS GOOD

Because God is good, the material universe God creates is good, and so is worth examining.

Christians had a positive attitude to matter. Christians also avoided two extremes: on the one hand, matter is not corrupt or evil; on the other hand, nature is not divine or the object of worship. So the world can become a subject for study. If the material universe were seen as corrupt or evil, we would have nothing to do with it. If the world was thought to be divine, to experiment with the world would be sacrilege. The doctrine that God created the world means that the world is somewhat autonomous and real and objective.

The Universe is Orderly

The universe is regular and orderly. It is not chaotic and unpredictable. If it were, it would make science impossible. The world behaves in a consistent and rational way; for example, liquids freeze at the same temperatures uniformly. Why is it like this? The universe is created by an intelligent Creator with a rational plan. Effects follow causes in a consistent way, and this is the basis of science.

The Universe could be Different

The universe is contingent. God is sovereign and free, and could have made the world very different from the way we find it. Its nature cannot be deduced from ideas, from first principles. The Greeks thought there was only one possible rational blueprint for the world, which could be discovered by **deduction**, theoretical reasoning, 'top down' thinking. They

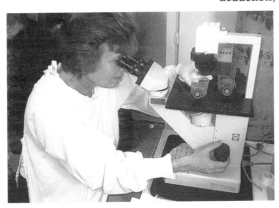

thought, in other words, that the world *had to be the way it was*. For the Greeks, the universe was necessary. A contingent world means we can only discover what it is like by **induction**; that is, by observation, analysis and testing of data, 'bottom up' thinking, the method of science.

The Universe is Understandable

The universe is intelligible to humans. The universe is not a closed book to us, but is open to our investigation. Why should we tiny humans on a minute planet have the ability to investigate the vast universe? Humans created in the image of God can understand the universe created by God. Our minds are 'tuned into' the universe. For example, mathematics, which is a human invention, is very mysteriously able to describe the physical world of nature, as Newton discovered. There is a fit between mathematical theory and the way the world works.

Objectivity, rationality, contingency and intelligibility of the natural world are the basic assumptions underlying science. These emerged originally from the Christian understanding of creation, and so favoured the rise of science. There is an argument, then, for claiming that Christian teaching, far from hindering the efforts of scientists, positively aided the growth of scientific thinking in the world.

THREE ANSWERS

Over the last four or five centuries, however, there has been a big question: Can science and religion contradict each other? There were, and are, three answers to the question. These answers are: 'Yes', 'No' and 'Maybe'.

The first answer is Yes. Science and religion can contradict each other. This is the **conflict theory** or the 'enemies relationship'. Science is more powerful, more objective and more truthful than religious teaching. As science discovers more, religion will be shown up as knowing less. To rely on science, and to abandon religious ideas, is true human progress. This belief is called **scientism**.

There is another kind of 'Yes', which is another example of the conflict theory. This time, it is the religion side that trumps science. Religion has the truth. This belief is called **fundamentalism**. This answer may be very comforting for a fundamentalist religious believer, but it ignores the real problems that scientific research and technological advances have raised for humanity today. The history of both science and religion shows that this answer is not very credible nowadays.

The second answer is No. Science and religion cannot really contradict each other; they only seem to. Each subject talks about different things. Science is concerned with the natural world, the universe, objective things and events. Religion is about the subjective life of the spirit, emotions, beliefs, hopes and fears. Each should stay on its own side of the line. This is called the **independence theory** or the 'separate domains relationship'.

The third answer is Maybe. Sometimes science can throw up a fact or theory that contradicts religious teaching. There is no quick, easy or routine way of deciding which is correct. It may be that the religious teaching is poorly understood and needs to be explored further, or it may be that the scientific statement needs revising or updating. Only open discussion between scientist and theologian can resolve such issues. This is called the **collaborative theory** or the 'dialogue relationship'.

We will now look at each answer in some more detail.

SCIENCE AND RELIGION ARE IN CONFLICT

Have you heard of Philip Pullman? He has written a striking trio of children's novels, called His Dark Materials. He is one of the most powerful children's writers today. But his story must be the most unusual one you could ever find in a child's book.

He tells a story of twelve-year-olds fighting to liberate all the many universes from an evil power called 'the church' (not a misprint!), which oppresses children and adults on behalf of 'the Authority' – a kind of devil-God.

In the second novel, the hero, Will Parry, is told by his father:

> 'Every little increase in human freedom has been fought over ferociously between those who want us to know more and be wiser and stronger, and those who want us to obey and be humble and submit.'

Pullman has summarised the conflict theory or enemies relationship between science and religion. He has the knack of expressing powerfully the emotion, the feeling and the motivation for secularists and humanists and other anti-religionists who charge the Church, theology and religion with keeping humans in captivity to ignorance and impotence.

HISTORY OF THE CONFLICT THESIS

August Comte (1798-1857) was probably the first and most famous writer to see science and religion as enemies. His central idea was the Law of Human Progress or the **Law of Three Stages**. As individuals, we grow up from the fairytales of childhood, through the critical period of teenage years, to the calm wisdom of adult life. In a similar way, Comte suggested that the human race has moved from the magical, fictitious, religious or theological stage, through the critical or abstract philosophical stage, to the scientific stage. Naturally enough, Comte identified the beginnings of the enlightened and scientific age with his own time.

Above:
August Comte
Right:
J. W. Draper

As the nineteenth century advanced, other thinkers picked up on the same idea. J.W Draper, for example, wrote an influential book called *History of the Conflict between Religion and Science*. The idea even ignited debate in Ireland. A Carlow man named John Tyndall contributed a celebrated Address to the British Society for the Advancement of Science at their Belfast meeting in 1874. He was a friend of many famous scientists of the period and had been elected President of the Society. In his Presidential Address, he argued for the superiority of scientific method over religious and philosophical doctrine for uncovering the secrets of the universe. The result was a lively controversy, as can well be imagined, given the city that hosted the speech. By the way, John Tyndall was the man who first explained why the sky is blue!

Above:
Richard Dawkins
Right:
John Tyndall

Modern proponents of the conflict theory are Richard Dawkins and Peter Atkins. Both of them are famous scientists in England, and both are often seen on the television. In the case of Richard Dawkins, this is to be expected, as he is the Professor of the Public Understanding of Science at Oxford University. Dawkins has written extensively on the process of biological evolution. He claims that science satisfactorily explains the existence of the universe and the emergence of life. He has no need for the hypothesis of God. For Dawkins, religion is an alternative to science and an illogical, ignorant and dangerous option. He is on record as opposing religion because it misleads people, devalues people and, ultimately, destroys people. Dawkins maintains that a scientific understanding is realistic, accurate and valuable. Like Philip Pullman, he thinks that religion is oppressive and he wants to liberate human beings from its clutch.

SCIENCE AND RELIGION ARE INDEPENDENT

By any stretch of the imagination, Stephen Jay Gould was an exciting scientist. Born in New York city in the 1940s, he, like many youngsters of his time, was fascinated by the huge dinosaur skeletons on display in the American Museum of Natural History. He decided then and there to spend his life discovering and digging up these fantastic extinct creatures. He finished his PhD from Columbia University in 1967, and eventually became Professor of Geology and Zoology at Harvard University. He was a controversial speaker and a prolific writer. Unfortunately, Stephen Jay Gould died unexpectedly in 2002.

Stephen Jay Gould

In his book *Rock of Ages*, Stephen Jay Gould explained his idea of the relationship between science and religion. He thought they should keep out of each other's way, coexist peacefully and not annoy each other. Neither science nor religion has any business fighting with each other, as they are about totally different things. Science is about the natural world, religion is about the moral world, and one has nothing to do with the other. Science should respect religion and ignore it, and religion should do the same with science. Science and religion are meant to be academic strangers, neither partners nor enemies.

Stephen Jay Gould was arguing for the independence theory or the 'relationship based on separate domains'. He had an acronym (a short word based on the initial letters of a longer title) for his position: he called his solution NOMA, for non-overlapping *magisteria*. (*Magisterium* is the Latin word for 'teaching' and *magisteria* is the plural 'teachings'.) NOMA allows both to proceed totally separately and peacefully.

Karl Barth

The great twentieth-century Swiss Protestant theologian, Karl Barth, was also of the opinion that religion and science should stay well apart. His reason was different from Stephen Jay Gould's. Barth believed that God is so much transcendent from the world, that religious truth is on a different plane from scientific truth. He insisted on a strict separation of science from theology. Scientific methods, he believed, are not suitable for theology. We cannot find out anything about God from nature, for example, and so natural theology is impossible. That is the domain of science, and theologians should stay out of it.

Separation of science and religion has the advantage of avoiding any conflict. But it ignores the actual history of science and religion. It also ignores the desire that human beings have to unite their knowledge. It is natural to ask the question: what difference would that make to something else? For instance, what difference does the scientific account of the origin of the universe make to the Christian doctrine of the creation of the world? That is a perfectly natural question, one would think, which anyone would want to discuss.

SCIENCE AND RELIGION ARE COLLABORATIVE

Sometimes, science and religion present different explanations for the same thing. Science says that the universe began thirteen billion years ago with the 'Big Bang'. A long period of expansion and evolution marked the development of the physical world and the emergence of sentient and intelligent life. Religion, as represented by the book of Genesis, says that God created the world by God's word alone, and that all the different species, including human beings, and the range of creatures with which we are familiar, came into being instantaneously.

A way of accounting for the competing explanations is to describe them as different 'maps' or 'models' of the same reality. This is the essence of the collaborative theory or dialogue relationship between science and religion.

DIFFERENT EXPLANATIONS

A way of thinking of different explanations is to think of them as maps or models.

A **map** is a schematic diagram indicating the principal features of an area, to enable one to grasp the essential relationships and important realities necessary for understanding it. For example, if you want to travel from Dublin to Cork, a road-map will indicate the best route, showing turns and corners, forks, side roads, towns and counties through which you will pass. Roads will be indicated by black lines, mountains by brown or red patches, villages and towns by large or small spots. We know that the real things are quite different, but these symbols are representations. They show us what is north and what is south, how far one feature is from another, and so they help to get us on our way.

But there are other kinds of map. In your Geography book, there might be an economic map, or a map of physical or geological details, or a map showing the different kinds and patterns of weather. Each of these displays a different aspect of the area between Dublin and Cork. One is not right, and the others wrong. They provide separate pictures and different information. We must put them together to compare what each is saying to us. They must interact with one another. We must dialogue about them.

A **model** is a small-sized representation, a copy, or a pattern of a larger reality. It is meant to let us examine, understand and, maybe, construct a full version. It is a comparison drawn between something familiar and a more complex thing that we are trying to understand. It is a 'visual aid', similar to a map.

Scientists use models quite a lot. The 'Big Bang', for example, is a commonly used model. It suggests that one way to imagine the early seconds and minutes of the beginning universe is to imagine it as a huge explosion.

Another such model is the depiction of atomic particles, nuclei, electrons, protons and so on, as tiny whirling billiard-balls rotating and circling around one another. A moment's thought will show you that the model cannot be strictly true. An atomic particle (smaller than any material thing we can see or directly observe) could plainly not resemble anything as solid as a billiard-ball, but for help in understanding, the simple is best.

The collaborative theory or dialogue relationship accepts that there will be different ways of explaining things, just as we have different maps or models for different ways of understanding and working with reality. But it does not assume that these are entirely separate and totally independent ways. They may relate to one another, they cover the same area, and they may have to come to some kind of reconciliation.

AREAS OF COLLABORATION

There are two areas of particular interest in the possible collaboration and reconciliation between science and religion. The first area is that of **'limit questions'**; that is, problems and puzzles that turn up on the boundaries between science and religion. Examples would be the question Albert Einstein raised: why is the world intelligible in the first place? Or the question of purpose: why is there a universe at all? The second area of interest is the **'consonance question'**; that is, the places where science and religion seem to support each other. An example of consonance is the question of scientific and religious methods: the use of maps and models, metaphors and analogies.

Scientists tend to use maps and models. Theologians and philosophers use metaphors and analogies. A **metaphor** is a kind of comparison of one reality to another. So we say, God is a 'Spirit'. The word 'Spirit' means 'Breath', the air drawn in and out of our lungs so many times each minute. It is the most insubstantial material reality we can imagine, and yet, without breathing, we will die very quickly. Breath is vital to life.

Assignment

Outline clearly the three options for the science and religion relationship. What is the essence of the collaborative theory?

Resources for further study
See teacher's text on CD-Rom for further suggestions.

This topic is also considered in Section A, The Search for Meaning and Values; Section B, Christianity: Origins and Contemporary Expressions; Section C, World Religions; Section G, Worship, Prayer and Ritual and Section I, Religion: The Irish Experience.

Karl Rahner

172

Hence, it is a good way of describing the non-material, invisible and yet necessary nature of God's reality. An **analogy** is a formal comparison, specifying the similarities and dissimilarities involved in the two things being compared.

Those who argue for the collaborative theory hope that science and religion, using similar methods of maps, models, metaphors and analogies, can be intellectual partners, and not enemies. They argue that science and religion are not all that different in their ways. Both try to express difficult concepts in concrete language, both have different ways of referring to the same world, and therefore both scientist and theologian should be talking to each other, looking for points of contact, areas of overlap, and parallel enquiries. The collaborative theory is the reason that we have been studying the relationship between science and religion in this course.

Of course, having studied the subject and read the history and thought about the issues, you are now able to make up your own mind. That is exactly where we should leave you and why we stop now. But here is a final thought that may indicate where God fits into our picture of the world.

GOD IS THE HORIZON

The ancient astronomers learned a trick for seeing faraway and dim objects. They had to star-gaze without telescopes or binoculars or any kind of lens, so they relied only on the naked eye. They found out that if you look a little bit to the side of the object you want to see, it will come into focus a bit better. This is a good way of understanding God's relationship with the universe. God is the horizon, the frame, the backdrop, the awareness at the edge of our experience of everything else. We notice God when our attention is directed on something else.

We exist because God is. As St Paul quoted in Athens, 'In him, we live and move and have our being.' A difficulty with understanding God is that it becomes very easy to slip God into the world again alongside everything else. We can easily forget that God is totally different from any creature.

Karl Rahner, a German Catholic theologian, imagines God to be the permanent presence to the world, but not in the world. When we become aware of ourselves or conscious of other things, we become conscious as well of the mystery that surrounds the world. The picture, so to speak, comes into focus simultaneously with the frame. The frame fades away into the beyond, the horizon of God.

We cannot locate God geographically, time God historically, measure God materially, touch God, taste God, smell God, listen for God or observe God. We cannot even adequately think about God. The instruments of thought and reason break down when applied to God. God is always inviting us onward into the future and into the beyond.

Revision of Important Terms

Look up the following terms which you have come across in this chapter and briefly explain each one. Each of these terms is printed in bold in the text.

Deduction, Induction, Conflict theory, Scientism, Fundamentalism, Independence theory, Collaborative theory, Law of Three Stages, Map, Model, Limit questions, Consonance question, Metaphor, Analogy.

In summary...

We identified several Christian attitudes that support a scientific outlook: that the universe is good, orderly, contingent and understandable.

We reviewed the three stances that people have taken on the science and religion debate: the conflict theory, the independence theory and the collaborative theory.

The collaborative theory is the basis for this book and this option in the Leaving Certificate. Collaboration requires that we seek areas for discussion that are open to both scientists and those interested in religion.

One such area is the question of language: scientists and theologians both use metaphors and analogies, models and maps. This is an example of a consonance question: where science and religion seem to support each other. Another area is that of limit questions, which deal with the boundaries between science and religion.

Throughout the consideration of science and religion, we have noticed a range of views about God. God could be immanent and active in the world, as for theism. God could be seen as more transcendent, as for deism. Finally, God could be seen as the horizon, as for Karl Rahner. Each of these has consequences for our view of the relationship between science and religion.